Real-Life
CRIMES
...and how they were solved

CHANCELLOR
PRESS

First published in Great Britain in 1994 by Chancellor Press
an imprint of Reed Consumer Books Limited
Michelin House
81 Fulham Road
London SW3 6RB
and Auckland, Melbourne, Singapore and Toronto

by arrangement with Eaglemoss Publications Ltd

The material in this book first appeared in partwork form

ISBN 1 85152 488 6

A CIP catalogue record for this book is available at the British Library

Printed and bound in China
Produced by Mandarin Offset

Picture acknowledgements

Front cover: *(main)* Rex Features; *(left)* Solo Syndication; *(centre)* Midsummer Books; *(right)* Rex Features. **5:** Anglia Press Agency/Express Newspapers. **6:** Solo Syndication/Anglia Press Agency/Anglia Press Agency. **6-7:** Solo Syndication. **7:** Express Newspapers/Syndication International/Anglia Press Agency. **8:** Anglia Press Agency/Anglia Press Agency/Midsummer Books/Syndication International. **9:** Express Newspapers/Midsummer Books/Anglia Press Agency/Anglia Press Agency. **10:** Anglia Press Agency/Midsummer Books/Midsummer Books. **11:** Anglia Press Agency/Syndication International/Midsummer Books. **12:** Solo Syndication/Anglia Press Agency/Anglia Press Agency/Anglia Press Agency. **13:** ZEFA/Roger W. Vargo – Los Angeles Daily News/Los Angeles Daily News. **14:** Los Angeles Daily News/UPI Bettman. **15:** Los Angeles Daily News. **16:** Los Angeles Daily News. **16-17:** Los Angeles Daily News. **17:** Los Angeles Daily News/Los Angeles Daily News/Los Angeles Daily News. **18:** Los Angeles Daily News. **19:** Los Angeles Daily News/Frank Spooner/Los Angeles Daily News. **20:** Los Angeles Daily News/Los Angeles Daily News. **22:** Los Angeles Daily News. **23:** Los Angeles Daily News/ZEFA/Los Angeles Daily News. **24:** Solo Syndication/Press Association/Solo Syndication/Syndication International. **25:** Topham Picture Source/Press Association. **26:** Solo Syndication/Syndication International/Syndication International/Topham Picture Source. **27:** UPI Bettman/Rex Features. **28:** Topham Picture Source/UPI Bettman/John Frost/John Frost. **29:** Rex Features/Rex Features/Rex Features/UPI Bettman. **30:** Topham Picture Source (five). **31:** UPI Bettman/UPI Bettman/Rex Features. **32:** UPI Bettman. **33:** UPI Bettman/UPI Bettman/Syndication International. **34:** UPI Bettman/UPI Bettman. **35:** Topham Picture Source/Paul Popper/UPI Bettman. **36:** Syndication International. **37:** Syndication International (three). **38:** Syndication International/Hulton Deutsch. **39:** Topham Picture Source. **40:** Syndication International. **41:** Topham Picture Source/Syndication International/Syndication International. **42:** Hulton Deutsch/Popperfoto/Hulton Deutsch. **43:** Topham Picture Source/Topham Picture Source/UPI Bettman. **44:** UPI Bettman (three). **45:** UPI Bettman/AP/Wideworld Photos/UPI Bettman/AP/Wideworld Photos/UPI Bettman. **46:** AP/Wideworld Photos/UPI Bettman. **47:** UPI Bettman (two). **48:** UPI Bettman (three). **49:** Topham Picture Source/Syndication International. **50:** Popperfoto/Midsummer Books/Syndication International. **50-1:** Hulton-Deutsch Collection. **51:** Syndication International/Popperfoto. **52:** Hulton-Deutsch Collection/Popperfoto. **52-3:** Topham Picture Source. **53:** Syndication International/Midsummer Books/Hulton-Deutsch Collection/Popperfoto. **54:** Syndication International/Popperfoto/Popperfoto/Midsummer Books. **55:** Popperfoto/Rex Features. **56:** Popperfoto/Popperfoto/Midsummer Books. **57:** Topham Picture Source/Kobal Collection/Syndication International/Topham Picture Source. **58:** John Topham Picture Source/Fall River Historical Society. **59:** Fall River Historical Society/Hulton Deutsch. **60:** John Topham Picture Source/John Topham Picture Source/John Topham Picture Source/Hulton Deutsch. **61:** Fall River Historical Society/Topham Picture Source. **62:** British Library/Fall River Historical Society/Fall River Historical Society. **63:** Popperfoto/Black Museum. **64:** Midsummer Books/Midsummer Books/Popperfoto/Popperfoto. **65:** Syndication International/Popperfoto/Popperfoto. **66:** Syndication International/Popperfoto/Syndication International. **68:** Popperfoto/Popperfoto/Black Museum/Popperfoto. **69:** Black Museum/Black Museum/Popperfoto. **70:** Popperfoto/Syndication International/Syndication International/Syndication International/Popperfoto. **71:** Syndication International/John Frost/Popperfoto. **72:** Syndication International. **73:** Syndication International. **74:** Syndication International/Syndication International. **74-5:** Popperfoto. **76:** Syndication International/Popperfoto/Syndication International. **77:** UPI Bettman/UPI Bettman. **78:** UPI Bettman. **79:** UPI Bettman.

CONTENTS

The Bamber Family

MURDERS

It seemed an open-and-shut case. The middle-class family had been killed in a fit of derangement by their beautiful adopted daughter, who then killed herself. Only the handsome son was left, grieving. At least, that was what everyone was supposed to think.

Above: A grieving Jeremy Bamber, well aware that he is in the viewfinders of Britain's press photographers, weeps at the funeral service for the members of his family, brutally slain at White House Farm.

Right: The Bamber family, in happier days, celebrate the Queen's Silver Jubilee. June and Nevill Bamber flank Sheila, young Jeremy, and Sheila's then-husband Colin Caffell.

At 3.36 a.m. on the morning of 7 August 1985, a telephone call buzzed on the switchboard of the police station at Chelmsford, Essex.

A frightened young man, farmer's son Jeremy Bamber, pleaded for help. "My father's just called. My sister has gone off her head – and she's got a gun," he told the duty officer.

At first the officer thought it was a hoax call from a local drunk: if it was a real emergency, a normal person would surely dial 999 rather than ring the more complicated number of a police station. Nevertheless

he radioed for the nearest patrol car to go to the small, pretty village of Tolleshunt d'Arcy.

Horrific scene

There the first officer on the scene met 25-year-old Jeremy Bamber at the gates of his parents' 18th-century farmhouse, White House Farm. He said, "My sister's a nutter. I think something terrible has happened. There are guns inside." Detectives were summoned, and tried ringing the farm. The phone was off the hook. The

police hesitated to enter the farmhouse for fear that the girl was armed and might shoot at them, but after four hours the decision was taken to go in.

They were confronted by a scene of sheer horror. Five people, including two little boys, lay dead, their bodies riddled with bullets. In the kitchen lay 61-year-old farmer and ex-RAF pilot Nevill Bamber, with eight bullet wounds in his head and body.

In the doorway of their daughter's bedroom, his wife June, also 61, lay on the floor. She had been sprayed with nine bul-

The procession of family coffins leaves the village church. Only the supposedly grieving Jeremy was left alive.

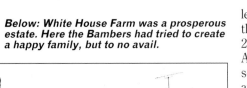

Sheila Caffell, Jeremy's sister, was an extremely attractive girl. Nicknamed 'Bambi', she could have been a top model except for her emotional instability.

Below: White House Farm was a prosperous estate. Here the Bambers had tried to create a happy family, but to no avail.

lets, one directly between her eyes. On the bed was the body of Jeremy's sister, 27-year-old former model Sheila Caffell. Across her lay a German-made Anschutz semi-automatic .22 rifle, its barrel pointing at the two bullet wounds in her throat. One shot had severed her jugular vein; the other had powered up into her skull, causing massive brain damage.

But, most heartbreaking of all, Sheila's six-year-old twin sons lay murdered in their beds. They had been shot as they slept – Daniel five times in the back of his head, and Nicholas despatched with three rounds.

Veteran detectives wept at the sight. And it may have been their tears that blinded them to the real facts about the massacre at White House Farm.

Within hours they had concluded that Sheila Caffell had gone off her head, wiped out her entire family, and then turned the gun on herself. She had a history of mental problems and drug abuse, and was known to be depressed. With Jeremy supplying the details of his sister's history of mental illness, while bravely staving off his grief for his slaughtered family, it seemed a classic murder/suicide tragedy.

The police had found no sign that anyone else had been at the house on that terrible night. All the windows and doors had been locked from the inside, and the police had had to force their way in.

The coroner's verdict was that of murder and suicide, and the bodies were released for burial; Jeremy, racked with grief, was photographed by newspapers at his parents' funeral.

But by this time relatives and friends of the Bamber family were sure that there was a far more sinister explanation, although their suspicions were dismissed by police. Most of all, Bamber's girlfriend Julie Mugford, then a 22-year-old trainee teacher, was filled with unease.

She knew that Bamber had harboured a barely hidden hatred for his whole family. He had talked endlessly about getting his hands on the family fortune of almost £500,000. Once they were dead, he had whooped it up on champagne, drugs and parties. And, within days of the killings, he had actually boasted, "It was all down to me. I paid a hitman two grand to do it. Now everything will pass to me."

High living

His behaviour did not ring true for a man whose whole family had just been wiped out. While other relatives mourned, he took Julie on a high-spending holiday to Amsterdam, smuggled cannabis home in toothpaste tubes, drank champagne and bought suits at £500 a time. He took over his sister's London flat and then tried to sell an album of her modelling photographs, including some soft porn material, to Sunday newspapers, demanding a four-figure sum. The papers turned him down.

Julie became more and more frightened by her boyfriend's bizarre behaviour and made the agonising decision to talk to the police. What she had to tell them eventually ran to 140 pages. Meanwhile, other clues had come to light, and the CID was forced to look at the case afresh.

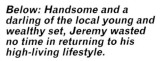

As the evidence against
Jeremy Bamber piled up,
detectives were able to
piece together the story of
what must have really
taken place that night.

Jeremy's Dark Secret

The weapon that caused such carnage at
White House Farm was a semi-automatic
Anschutz .22-calibre rifle with a 10-shot
magazine. German-made, the Anschutz
could be fitted with a silencer.

In the small hours of 7 August, when the family were asleep, Bamber went to his parents' home. He travelled by bike so that no-one would see his car. He slipped on gloves and silently entered the house, using a hacksaw blade to force a lavatory window after the family had gone to bed.

Like many farmers, Nevill Bamber kept a locked gun cabinet. His son knew where to find the key. The cabinet contained several shotguns, but there was also a 10-shot, .22 automatic rifle with a silencer.

Bamber had used the gun many times. His father had bought it to control the rabbits that infested the farm; the silencer had been added later so that he could shoot rabbits without frightening the others back into their warrens.

Detectives believe that Bamber had just loaded a 10-round magazine into the gun and screwed on the silencer when he was confronted by his father. Nevill Bamber was six feet four inches in height, fit, and

powerfully built. Bamber shot him in cold blood. As he slumped to his knees, wounded, Bamber mercilessly battered him with the gun, swinging it like a club. He hit his father so hard that the rifle stock broke. Then, as he slumped on to the floor, Bamber pumped four more shots into his head.

Shooting spree

With icy indifference Bamber collected two more ammunition clips from the cupboard, reloaded, and went upstairs. He walked into his parents' bedroom and sprayed bullets at his mother as she attempted to get out of bed. She was hit in the knee, arm, twice in the chest, at the base of her neck and at the side of her head.

Bamber then made his way down the corridor to his sister's room, where she slept undisturbed by the silenced shots. This one had to look like suicide. Bamber placed the gun muzzle under her chin and pulled the trigger. Sheila died instantly. ▶

At this point police believe that Mrs Bamber, in her death throes, had crawled from her room to the doorway of her daughter's bedroom. Bamber put the barrel to her forehead and finished her off with a point-blank shot between the eyes. Again he reloaded, and went into the room where his nephews slept. He shot them too.

Finally, Bamber stepped over the body of his mother to re-enter his sister's room. Police think he had already removed the silencer from the gun at the end of his shooting spree but then decided to make sure that his sister was dead by shooting her again. He then pressed her hand against the gun after wiping off his own fingerprints. But he was not as thorough as he thought – one of his prints remained on the trigger, another vital clue that was missed at first.

Bogus call

Before leaving the scene, Bamber lay the gun across Sheila's body with the barrel pointing towards the bullet holes in her neck, to reinforce the impression that her death was suicide.

He drove to his home, a farm cottage three miles away in the village of Goldhanger, and after a couple of hours made his bogus alarm call to the police.

More than 40 detectives, photographers and forensic specialists came to the farm the next day. If anyone suspected then that it was not such a clear-cut matter, no-one voiced it, even though one detective noticed how strange it was that Jeremy Bamber could calmly cook himself a breakfast of toast and fried bacon while the bodies of his entire family were being examined only five miles away.

The police thought that this was an open-and-shut case; they read the situation exactly as Jeremy Bamber had intended them to. It seemed clear that Sheila Caffell had killed the family and then turned the gun on herself.

The first doubts

But two days after the killings, Nevill and June Bamber's nephew David Boutflour, also a farmer, went to the farm. He looked in his uncle's gun cupboard and noticed a silencer, which he recognised as being for a .22 rifle, the gun used in the murders. Handling it with great care, he saw congealed blood inside and realised that it must have come from one of the victims. Also, there were red paint marks on the outside, implying that it must have been scraped against something, and sticking to it was a single hair.

The police had taken the rifle – why had they not taken the silencer? Eventually, after Bamber's girlfriend had gone to the police and more forensic evidence gradually came to light, Jeremy Bamber became

The road to murder

Jeremy Bamber's road to murder started long before 1985. He was an arrogant, heartless person, who obviously felt that the world owed him the resources necessary to live in the style he desired. He had talked for some time about getting rid of the obstacles in the way of his inheritance. People felt it was just talk, but in August 1985 the handsome young killer set into motion a carefully worked out plan for personal enrichment, a plan that would require careful timing and could only come about with the brutal murder of his adoptive parents and sister and her two young sons.

Above left: Jeremy Bamber was employed by his father as manager on White House Farm, but he did not like the work and thought the salary was derisory.

Below: Jeremy lived in the village of Goldhanger, about three miles west of White House Farm.

Above: Jeremy Bamber's home was a former farm cottage, owned by the Bambers, and came with his job on White House Farm.

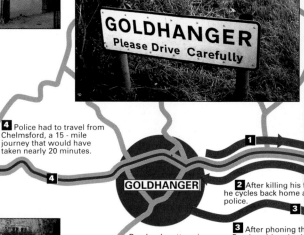

From Chelmsford

4 Police had to travel from Chelmsford, a 15 - mile journey that would have taken nearly 20 minutes.

GOLDHANGER

1

2 After killing his he cycles back home a police.

3

3 After phoning th Bamber drives back White House Farm.

Bamber 's cottage in Goldhanger belonged to his father's estate.

5 Police overtake B way to the farm have taken only fi set off immediate vital po

Left: Police search Bamber's car. He did not drive to the farm when he committed the murders, preferring to avoid observation by riding his bike through the country lanes.

a suspect and was arrested six weeks after the shootings. In the early stages, however, all these major points had been missed:

☐ The police overtook Jeremy Bamber on the road to White House Farm. They had travelled 15 miles from Chelmsford; Jeremy's journey from his home would have taken five minutes at most. Why had he not hurried off immediately after phoning the police?

☐ The silencer was still in the gun cupboard. When the police finally collected it – two days later – they lost the hair that was sticking to it.

☐ The red paint on the silencer matched scrape marks on a mantelpiece in the kitchen, where Nevill Bamber had died after a violent struggle.

☐ The blood in the silencer had come from Sheila. She could not have fired the gun AND placed the muzzle under her chin with the silencer in place – her arms were too short.

☐ Powder marks around the wounds showed that one shot had been fired with a silencer and the other without. How could Sheila have shot herself once and then removed the silencer before the second shot – and how in any case could she have shot herself twice, when the first shot would have been fatal?

TOLLESHUNT D'ARCY

TOLLESHUNT D'ARCY

cycles from his
...ldhanger to
... Farm.

The Bambers were
prominent
members of
Tolleshunt d'Arcy
society and the
church.

4

1

The Bamber family
lived together at
White House Farm -
and together they
met there deaths
there.

3

2

on their
...y would
...he had
...ing the
...missed.

5

WHITE HOUSE FARM

Above: Police vehicles gather in the yard at the back of White House Farm on the morning after the murders.

Above: Nevill Bamber was shot and battered to death in the kitchen. His wife June was shot in bed.

Right: Victim Sheila Caffell and her twin sons. The two boys were shot repeatedly in a vicious and heartless attack.

Reconstruction

Left: Pathological evidence pointed to the use of a silencer. Why did the police fail to search for such a device?

Jeremy Bamber cycled down back lanes to commit his crimes. That way no-one would see him.

He entered the house using a hacksaw blade on a lavatory window. How did police miss these signs of forced entry?

Jeremy used his father's rifle to kill his family, and then returned home to telephone the police.

Bamber lived less than three miles away, yet the Chelmsford police overtook his car and arrived at the farm first.

▶ ☐ Sheila was supposed to have walked around the house murdering her family. There was a lot of blood – but Sheila's feet were spotlessly clean.

☐ Sheila knew nothing about guns. Jeremy, on the other hand, was a crack shot.

☐ The murder weapon was well oiled, but there was no gun oil or grease on Sheila's hands or nightgown. Nor were there any signs of powder burns.

☐ The release catch for the rifle magazine was so stiff that a police ballistics expert broke a fingernail trying to release it. Sheila's beautifully manicured nails showed no sign of damage.

☐ Nevill Bamber was a powerful man, nearly six feet four in height. How could Sheila, at five feet seven and weighing only eight stone, have battered him into submission with enough force to break the rifle stock?

☐ The murder weapon was moved during the photography of the murder scenes, and officers did not wear gloves while handling it.

☐ One of the cartridge cases was not found until two days later, under a wardrobe.

☐ Jeremy Bamber had supposedly been at his own home when he rang the police, when he reported that his father had telephoned to say that Sheila was running amok. But at the farmhouse the phone was off the hook. This meant that Jeremy's phone would still have been connected to the farmhouse, and he would not have been able to make a call. If he wasn't at home when he rang the police, where was he?

☐ A lavatory window bore marks where Bamber had forced it open to get into the farmhouse. No-one noticed them at the time.

☐ Bamber had used a hacksaw to prise open the window. He dropped it on the ground outside, but it was not found for another two months.

☐ Because the family were allowed access to the farmhouse only two days

Pillars of Society

The Bambers were pillars of society in the tiny Essex village of Tolleshunt d'Arcy. Nevill Bamber was a local magistrate; his wife was a churchwarden. They were unable to have children, and had adopted both Sheila and Jeremy through the Church of England Children's Society. Relations with both children were difficult – Sheila led a turbulent life and had a history of mental problems, but they managed to remain on reasonable terms with her although they disapproved of her lifestyle. At the time of the killings she had taken refuge with them after her divorce.

Jeremy was different. He had grown up hating both his parents, and made no secret of it. His greed and callousness led to tragedy.

Top: Nevill Bamber was an influential man, whose standing in the local community was unquestioned.

Right: A plaque commemorates Nevill and June Bamber at their local church, where June was a churchwarden.

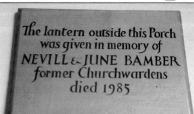

The lantern outside this Porch was given in memory of NEVILL & JUNE BAMBER former Churchwardens died 1985

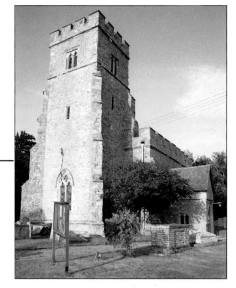

after the murders, Jeremy was able to take away bloodstained carpets and bedding and burn them. These could have contained vital forensic evidence.

☐ Bamber was not even fingerprinted until six weeks after the killings. One of his prints was found on the gun's trigger. ▶

The phone at the farm was off the hook. Jeremy could therefore not have been at home when he telephoned the police, since his phone would still have been connected to the farm.

Such calm, callous behaviour should have surprised the police officers accompanying him.

After leaving the farm in the hands of the investigators, Bamber went home, where he cooked and ate a fry-up with every evidence of enjoyment.

Police possibly thought they were acting sensitively, but surely the material from the house should have undergone a thorough forensic examination?

Jeremy insisted that he could not face the inside of the farmhouse with signs of carnage everywhere, and asked for carpets and bedding to be burned.

Bambi's tragedy

Sheila Caffell, Jeremy's sister, was the child of an illicit affair between the teenage daughter of a chaplain in Canterbury and a young curate. As she grew up with her adoptive parents she, like her brother, kicked against their middle-class values and June Bamber's almost fanatic religious beliefs – she had apparently once called her ''the Devil's daughter'' after catching her and a boyfriend together.

After leaving home to go to college she started using drugs and earned money as a glamour model. Nicknamed 'Bambs' by the family and known as Bambi in the modelling world, she married, but had gone through a difficult divorce shortly before the family was murdered. She was known to be depressed, and continued to be mentally unstable: during psychiatric treatment she had told her therapist that she suspected her twins of trying to seduce her. All this, plus her history of drug abuse, helped to bolster Jeremy's story that she had killed her parents and children and then turned the gun on herself.

Sheila Caffell's emotional instability was well known in the village. Jeremy Bamber used his adopted sister's mental problems to cover his own crime, misleading the police into thinking that Sheila had committed the murders in a fit of mania.

Sheila Caffell was supposed to have committed suicide by shooting herself through the neck. But with a silencer the barrel was far too long for her to have reached the trigger.

The caravan break-in

Jeremy Bamber had a small share in the family caravan site overlooking the Blackwater estuary. This did not stop him robbing the place.

After Julie Mugford went to the police with her story, six weeks after the murders, the Essex police decided to question Jeremy Bamber. He was arrested at his flat in Maida Vale – the flat that had been his sister's. Taken to Chelmsford for questioning, he denied that he had anything to do with the killings. However, he admitted to a burglary at the family caravan park at Maldon in March, five months before the carnage at White House Farm, when nearly £1,000 had been stolen. As a diversionary measure his confession seemed to work, since he was released on bail. He immediately headed south for a jet-set holiday on the French Riviera.

For the love of Jeremy

Above and right: Jeremy Bamber had an undoubted attraction for women. At the funeral of his family, it was girlfriend Julie Mugford who stood by him. A year later, she was to be the prosecution's key witness against him in court.

Robert and Pamela Boutflour were Jeremy Bamber's uncle and aunt. It was their son David who would not believe Sheila Caffell was capable of such a brutal crime, and who helped piece together the vital evidence.

POSTSCRIPT
Jeremy's penfriend

Bamber's girlfriend Julie Mugford once told a friend that the mass murderer she had once loved was "the Devil incarnate". He quickly revealed his all-consuming hatred for his family to her. She later told police that her lover came up with "plot after plot after plot" for doing away with them. She said: "He thought his parents were old fools standing in the path of his inheritance.

"He resented his sister for having a £20,000 per year allowance to have a flat in west London. He hated her twin sons, saying they would be a further problem in the way of him getting his hands on the family money.

"He had it all worked out; he knew to the pound how much they were worth. He talked openly about shooting them and then burning down the house to conceal the crime. When talking about it once he changed his mind and said that was a bad plan, because there were valuables in the house he could sell after they were all dead and he would lose those if there was a fire.

"Thoughts of getting rid of his family dominated his life."

At first, deeply in love with Bamber, Julie dismissed all this as fantasy. Then, the night before he went on his killing spree, Bamber rang Julie at her flat in Lewisham and said, "Tonight's the night." After the murders he told her that he had planned the killings and had paid a hitman to carry them out. She still did not dream that he meant it. But his continuing bizarre and callous behaviour, immediately after the death of his closest family, all became too much for her, and she went to the police.

Even after he was charged with five murders, Jeremy Bamber retained his attraction for women. Before his arrest, he had developed a new relationship with beautician Anji Greaves. They exchanged more than 100 letters while he was on remand.

David Boutflour said after the trial: "We felt there was a difference of opinion among the detectives themselves about the case. Some of them thought there was more to it, but some of the senior officers thought it was a 'domestic'.

"Sheila was a lovely girl. When we went back to the farm we got this feeling that they were all still alive and telling us somehow to look for something else. We just felt that the whole thing did not add up."

Arrested and tried

One officer on the inquiry admitted later: "It was highly embarrassing. But the truth is people were forced to take notice of what they found that we missed. Together with one or two other things, they made the difference between Bamber getting away with it and inheriting the family fortune, and Bamber getting 25 years."

Bamber was arrested in London and questioned at Chelmsford police station for 18 hours. He denied the murders, but admitted that he had been responsible for an earlier burglary at the family's caravan park, where £980 had been stolen. He was charged with this offence and released on bail, and promptly went off on holiday to St Tropez.

The police carried on their investigation, and continued to turn up the forensic and circumstantial evidence that pointed to Jeremy Bamber. Six weeks after the massacre, he was arrested at Dover as he arrived back from holiday.

He went on trial at Chelmsford Crown Court in October 1986, pleading 'not guilty' to five charges of murder. But after a 19-day trial he was convicted, and is now serving five life sentences with a recommendation that he serves at least 25 years. □

JOE HUNT'S BILLIONAIRE BOYS' CLUB

Whizz-kids turn to
MURDER

Above: Joe Hunt, alias Joe Gamsky, went to Los Angeles from Chicago. Moving in fashionable circles, he befriended some of the richest families in California.

Right: Hunt's first victim was an ageing homosexual con-man called Ron Levin. He tricked Hunt in a bogus investment and was rewarded with a bullet in the head.

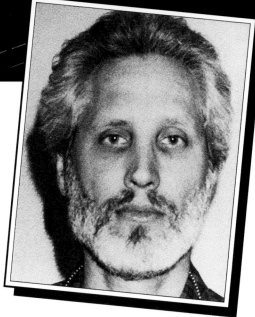

Joe Hunt was a brash young con-man who dreamed of making millions on the stock exchange. But when his plans failed, he turned to murder.

Joe Hunt ushered the 30 or so smart and fashionably dressed young men into the living room of his condominium in San Fernando Valley, Los Angeles. It was a warm evening in March 1983. Joe was 24, and his dream was about to be realised. These were the sons of the richest families in California, and they had come to listen to him, the gifted child of a poor family who'd moved west from Chicago in the 1960s.

He'd known most of them at school, when Joe had been the scholarship boy among the rich kids of exclusive Harvard Prep School. Mostly they'd looked down on him then as an outsider and a bit of a jerk. But now things were different.

Since school Joe had passed his accountancy exams at the age of just 19. He'd graduated from the University of Southern California, he claimed, after just 18

13

Victim

Battle of the con-men

Left: Outwardly Levin got along well with Joe Hunt, but he was secretly trying to get the better of Hunt in a series of crooked deals.

Right: Hunt was furious when he realised that Levin had managed to cheat him. He began to plan his revenge.

Ron Levin was born Ronald Glick on 16 February 1942. His father was killed during World War II, and the boy was brought up by his mother and stepfather. Thrown out of half-a-dozen schools before he was nine, Ronnie, as his doting mother called him, grew up to own a series of fly-by-night companies, selling anything from legal research to a 'Super Sex Catalogue', which went mail-order for $2.

A self-confessed 'thief', Ron spent several months in prison, and was facing 12 criminal charges at the time of his disappearance, including grand theft and receiving stolen property. However, he also moved happily among the famous, numbering Muhammad Ali, Bianca Jagger and Andy Warhol among his friends.

Body never found

Levin's body was never found, so the prosecution at Joe Hunt's trial for murder had first to prove he was dead. Levin's mother, Carol, testified that her dutiful son had phoned her at least once a week for the past 24 years, and would certainly have let her know if he was still alive. There was also the fact that no money had been removed from any of Levin's accounts since the date of his disappearance.

Witness doubted

On the other hand, a defence witness said she'd seen a man at a gas station in Arizona, whom she later recognised as Levin from a drawing in *Esquire* magazine. But Prosecutor Fred Wapner, through merciless cross-examination, succeeded in casting doubt on the identification.

Recent sighting

However, even after his conviction Hunt went on maintaining that Levin was still alive, and would turn up one day. There were at least five further reports of his having been seen alive, including one man who said he'd spoken to Levin in a queue for a film in Westwood, Los Angeles. Police pointed out that such false reports are extremely common in cases of missing persons.

Joe outlined the BBC ethos. He called it Paradox Philosophy. He told them they should look at any situation according to how it affected them, not other people. That way they wouldn't stand in the way of their own success. "By reorienting your perspective," Joe told them, "you can see almost anything in a completely different way."

He also outlined the structure of the organisation. There were special names for the leaders ('shadings'), projects ('shapes'), project leaders ('thraxes') and so on. In fact, the whole thing was very much like a child's fantasy. But the audience that night didn't think so. They liked the idea of being in charge of their own destiny. But mostly they were drawn by the tall, dark, charismatic young man who addressed them.

Regular cheat

In reality, however, Joe Hunt was not all that he seemed. At school he'd shown a propensity for bending the rules, when he got thrown off the debating team for cheating. Later he had dropped out of university, when his fraternity house, who had elected him president, objected to his dictatorial manner. Then his dreams of success as a commodities trader were shattered, when regulators in Chicago suspended him for the maximum 10 years. Once again he'd been breaking the rules.

Now Joe was flat broke. Even the condo belonged to his friend Dean Karny's parents. He had two real aims for the BBC. The first was to raise money to play the commodities market himself. The second, which was even more important to him, was to make himself what he'd always wanted to be – a leader. As he handed out his professionally produced prospectus, a leader is certainly what he looked to his yuppie audience that night. Before long Hunt would be exercising an extraordinary power over the group.

Keen investors

The Billionaire Boys' Club was soon in full swing. Twins Dave and Tom May, the sons of TV cowboy Ty Hardin, invested $80,000 each. Steve Weiss, the father of a friend of one BBC member, put in another $20,000 and, after Joe declared quick profits, started to recruit among his many friends.

Joe's method of attracting new money was simplicity itself. It was also fraud. An investor would put up an initial small sum – say $5,000. Within a month Joe would send back most of the money, saying it was profit from his trading. Sure that he was on to a winner, the investor would then put in a lot more money. Further 'profits' were continually promised, but none ever materialised.

months. He'd also been a commodities trader on the floor of the Chicago Mercantile Exchange. Now he had Brooke Roberts, attractive blonde daughter of record producer Bobby Roberts, living with him. In fact, Joe Hunt looked like a young man going places, while his privileged schoolfellows were still trying to find a way of establishing themselves independently of their wealthy families.

That evening Joe offered them a way of doing just that. He was proposing to start a business and social club. Its members, to be drawn exclusively from California's brightest and best, would pool resources to finance their own business schemes and trade commodities. They would be free of the adult world of big business, which refused, Joe told them, to take young people seriously.

The club was to be called the BBC after the Bombay Bicycle Club, Joe's favourite after-hours hang-out in Chicago. But its members soon took the initials and renamed the organisation the Billionaire Boys' Club.

Joe Hunt knew Ron Levin had a Swiss bank account and he believed Levin's claim that he was a millionaire. Hunt planned to make him sign over his fortune at gunpoint.

"Sign, or die"

1 Hunt invited himself to Levin's flat, bringing two salads with him!

2 Jim Graham arrived next, posing as a Mafia gunman.

3 Levin signed a cheque for $1.5 million and handed it over.

4 They then made Levin lie face down on the bed and Graham shot him.

5 They bundled his body up, wrapping the TV remote control in with him.

Joe Hunt thought that if Levin 'disappeared' people would assume he was fleeing from another failed con trick. But he vanished just before a planned trip to New York, and his housekeeper noticed the missing TV control which Levin always kept on the bed. Levin had a final laugh from beyond the grave: the cheque he was forced to sign at gunpoint bounced.

Obviously to keep the scam going Joe needed constant injections of new cash, especially after the BBC moved into smart and expensive new offices on 3rd Street in West Hollywood. One name that came up was that of Ron Levin, a 40-year-old homosexual, with a nice line in fraud himself.

Levin's most recent con had been to persuade Panasonic and RCA to lend him $130,000-worth of video equipment as props for a TV pilot about reporters gathering late-night news. He then proceeded to turn a tidy profit by actually gathering news footage, and selling it to local TV stations.

Ron Levin made no bones about his occupation. In fact, he boasted about it to friends and acquaintances. So Joe knew he was dealing with a fellow con-artist. He seems to have regarded it as a challenge. It was a fatal miscalculation – fatal, that is, for Ron Levin.

Levin took his time, enjoying having the handsome young Billionaire Boys around

his Beverly Hills apartment, while he and Hunt circled warily, each looking for a way to exploit the other. Then in June 1983 Levin agreed to allow Joe to trade at Clayton Brokerage with $5m of his money. Profits would be split 50/50 between Levin and the BBC.

Total disaster

It was almost a total disaster immediately. By the end of July Joe had lost all but $1m of Levin's money. He had also lost all of the May twins' money. Then suddenly he hit a winning streak on Levin's account.

Trading commodities consists of guessing whether the price of basic commodities and the value of currencies will rise or fall. All at once Joe Hunt could do no wrong. On 17 August, when Levin told him to liquidate all positions, Joe had run the account up to nearly $14m. His share of the profits was over $4m.

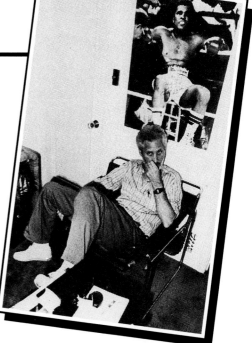

Ron Levin moved in equally fashionable circles in California. The boxer Mohammed Ali gave him a signed poster which had pride of place in his Beverly Hills apartment.

David May (left) and his twin brother Tom, photographed here for their school yearbook, were classmates of Joe Hunt at the exclusive Harvard Prep school. Tom May told his brother that Joe Hunt was boasting about his killing of Ron Levin, and the twins told their stepfather and his attorneys.

The BBC had really arrived. The May twins got their money back with interest, other investors were promised a bonus, and Joe and Brooke Roberts moved into a fancy new apartment in the Wilshire Manning complex. Joe's fellow 'shadings', Dean Karny and Ben Dosti, moved in with them. Then the whole house of cards fell down around their ears. Joe hadn't been trading with real money.

Back in June Levin had conned Clayton Brokerage that he was doing a story on trading for the TV news. He told them he wanted Clayton's to let a young broker trade a dummy account there in exchange for the free publicity. The only thing was that they mustn't let the young man know he wasn't using real money.

Levin's angle was that he could then take the impressive-looking account sheets from Clayton's, and use them to set up a real account elsewhere, without having to produce any money up front. The new account made Levin a nice profit, but Joe Hunt and the BBC were left with nothing.

Joe hid his feelings, pretending to remain friends with Levin, but inside he was seething. He told Dean Karny: "I'm going to kill Ron Levin one day." Events would prove that he wasn't kidding.

By the spring of 1984 the BBC was in deep financial trouble. Joe managed to squeeze yet another cash injection out of his trusting investors, but he was looking for another way to raise big money. Once again he turned to Ron Levin, but this time the plan was rather different. This plan would show just how far the high priest of Paradox Philosophy was prepared to go.

First Joe let it be known that Levin was planning to put money into a rock-crushing

machine to which the BBC owned the rights. He drew up fake documents and correspondence about the deal, making sure his secretary typed them, in case she was questioned later. Then he inveigled Levin round to the offices, and introduced him around. If Levin were to sign a cheque to the BBC now, no-one could doubt it was a legitimate business deal – even if Levin were mysteriously to disappear shortly afterwards.

Guns in the office

Joe Hunt began to spend more and more time closeted in his office with Jim Graham, ex-security guard at the Wilshire Manning, now the BBC's Head of Security. Guns started to appear around the offices. Most of the Billionaire Boys, who liked to hang out at the office, but never made any serious attempt to do any business, thought the guns were just cool new accessory items. Then one evening Dean Karny came into Joe's office to find him poring over a list he'd made on some sheets of yellow legal notepaper. The list was headed: 'AT LEVIN'S: TO DO'. In court some three years later it would be called a "recipe for murder".

Levin had a trip to New York planned for 7 June. This, Joe believed, was his chance. If Ron disappeared now, no-one would miss him.

On the night of 6 June Joe picked up two take-out salads and took them over to Levin's house. At a pre-arranged time Jim Graham arrived at the front door. Joe let him in, and Graham produced the .25 Beretta he always kept strapped to his ankle. But this was no ordinary stick-up.

Graham held the gun on both men, while Joe made his pitch.

He told Levin he was in debt to the Mafia, and that Graham was their enforcer. If Levin didn't pay up for him now, they would both be killed. While Jim Graham held the gun on him, Levin signed a cheque for $1.5m against his Swiss bank account. At once both men turned on Levin. He was forced into the bedroom, and told to lie down on the bed. Then, as Levin lay face down on the white counterpane, Jim Graham shot him in the back of the head with the silenced Beretta.

A pit had already been dug out in Soledad Canyon, a remote area one hour north-east of Los Angeles. But before they drove the body there, Joe left some of his fake documents in the house. He wanted to be sure no-one would ask awkward questions about the cheque.

Out in Soledad Canyon they threw Levin's corpse into the hole, then blasted the face with a shotgun until it was un-identifiable. Recounting the story to Dean Karny later, Joe Hunt chuckled as he re-called a shotgun blast causing the dead man's brain to jump out of his skull, landing on the corpse's chest. The body was never found.

But Joe Hunt had reckoned without Levin's taste for company. Ron had

Guilty

Right: Joe Hunt took an active role in his defence, constantly passing notes to his legal team.

Hunt's evil henchmen

Ben Dosti and Dean Karny were the other two 'shadings' in the BBC and were also co-conspirators in the murder of Hedayat Eslaminia the following month. Ben and Dean were Hunt's contemporaries at Harvard Prep School, but neither had counted him as a friend. However, when they ran into six-feet four-inch Joe again in Westwood Village in the spring of 1980, both were impressed by his apparent transformation into a hugely self-confident man of business.

Conspiracy to murder

The Karny family were the first to invest in Joe Hunt's trading enterprises and, despite losing large sums of money, continued to believe in their son's friend right up to his arrest. Then Dean became the one to blow the whistle to the police, and testify against his ex-friends in court.

Ben Dosti's father had made a fortune in the aerospace industry in California. His mother wrote a highly influential column in the *Los Angeles Times* on food. They soon became suspicious of Hunt, but by then it was impossible to separate Ben from his hero.

Life sentences

Joe's two fellow-shadings became so convinced by Paradox Philosophy that they accepted the murder of Ron Levin as necessary, and were prepared actively to participate in the kidnap and murder of Eslaminia. Dean bought gags, handcuffs and disguises for 'Project Sam', as it was called, as well as two trunks. Ben was deputed to get air-freshener to mask the smell of chloroform and spray-on bandage to avoid leaving fingerprints. Ben Dosti and Reza Eslaminia received life sentences.

Left: Reza Eslaminia conspired with Joe Hunt to murder his own father and take his money.

Above: Like Reza, Ben Dosti is now serving a life sentence for second-degree murder.

planned to take two young men with him to New York. They arrived at the house next morning, and found no-one at home, so they called the housekeeper. She found the remains of two salads in the kitchen. She also found that Levin's white counterpane had been replaced with a green one, and that the TV remote control, which was always kept on the bed, was missing. She alerted the police.

But though Levin had apparently gone away without taking any clothes, the police decided there was nothing initially suspicious about his disappearance, and there the matter rested for some two months.

The last laugh

Meanwhile, from beyond the grave Ron Levin had the last laugh on Joe Hunt. The cheque bounced. With the money situation increasingly desperate and whispers of dis-satisfaction at BBC Headquarters growing louder, Joe decided on a new strategy. He would take selected trusted members of the organisation into his confidence, thereby, so he theorised, binding them more closely to him.

Ben and Dean had already been told of Levin's murder. Both had their morality so distorted by Paradox Philosophy that they agreed the killing had been justified. They

Guilty

Muscle man

Jim Pittman, alias Jim Graham, was Hunt's most trusted henchman. He shot Ron Levin and helped overpower Hedayat Eslaminia. But he was all muscle and no brains: after killing Levin he went on a spending spree in New York – using the credit cards of a con-man with a Jewish surname! Hunt had to fly to New York to bail him out.

A 28-year-old, streetwise, black security guard at the Wilshire Manning, Jim Graham impressed members of the BBC at a party in the complex by claiming to be an ex-Mr Universe, an ex-footballer with the Philadelphia Eagles and a karate black belt. Graham soon became the BBC's Director of Security and one of Joe Hunt's most trusted lieutenants.

Small-time crook

In reality he was a small-time criminal from Delaware, on the run from a theft warrant, and his real name was Jim Pittman. When things began to go wrong financially at the BBC, Hunt turned more and more to Jim, both as muscle and as a spy on Billionaire Boys he suspected of disloyalty.

After Levin's murder, Jim went on a spending spree in New York on the dead man's credit cards. Eventually when he'd overstepped Levin's credit limit, Jim was arrested under the name of Ron Levin for trying to leave without paying his hotel bill. Joe Hunt had to fly to New York to bail Graham out.

Tried twice for murder

Jim Pittman was tried twice for the murder of Ron Levin. Both times the jury was unable to agree on a verdict. Finally he was allowed to plead guilty to lesser charges and released, only to be re-arrested for the murder of Hedayat Eslaminia.

also thought some of the others would think the same way. So, with their agreement, as well as that of Jim Graham, on 24 June Joe called a meeting at the Wilshire

Manning for several BBC members.

Charismatic as ever, Joe Hunt had their attention from the start. He said he had something important to tell them about a

matter which "could be illegal", and that if they didn't want this "higher knowledge", they should leave. No-one moved. Then Joe dropped his bombshell. "Jim and I knocked off Ron Levin. We're also broke."

So completely were his followers under Joe's spell that no-one questioned him about the murder. In fact, they were far more concerned about the financial situation, and spent the rest of the meeting discussing new ways to raise money. But one young man at the meeting hadn't been sufficiently indoctrinated in Paradox Philosophy to accept what he heard.

Jeff Raymond went to his close friend Dave May and told him what Joe Hunt was claiming to have done. The two boys took their story to Dave's adopted father, 73-year-old tycoon David May II, who sent them to his lawyer. But the fact was that no-one could be sure if Joe was telling the truth. He'd lied often enough in the past. David May's attorneys advised the boys to stay in the BBC and find out all they could. It wasn't yet time to involve the police.

Iranian exile

Back in mid-June a 23-year-old Iranian boy, named Reza Eslaminia, had dropped some papers at the BBC HQ and got talking to Ben Dosti. Reza's father, Hedayat Eslaminia, had been a member of the Shah of Iran's government, and the family had been forced to flee after the revolution that brought Ayatollah Khomeini to power in 1978. But what made Ben's ears prick up was the $30m that Reza said his father had got out of the country. Ben took the Iranian boy to Joe Hunt.

Reza Eslaminia was exactly the kind of young man who fell most easily under Joe's spell. Groomed to be Prime Minister of Iran, then forced to leave for the US, where his estranged parents fought over him, Reza was soon in trouble with drugs. His father, whom Reza came to hate, was himself an opium addict and possibly on the hit-list for Khomeini's death squads.

Kidnap plot

It wasn't long before Joe and Reza, who was an eager disciple of Paradox Philosophy, had cooked up a scheme to kidnap Hedayat, and force him to sign over his money to his son. The Iranian's disappearance, they were sure, would be blamed on Khomeini or drug connections. It was Reza's own suggestion that once the transfer was made, they should then kill his father. They called the plan Project Sam.

There was no time to lose. Hedayat was planning a trip to Europe, and besides, the BBC needed fresh capital urgently. A secluded house on Beverly Glen Boulevard, off Sunset Boulevard, was found. There Eslaminia could be held, and his cries under torture would not be heard.

The real-estate agent who rented the house out remembered two well-dressed young men, the taller of whom (Hunt himself) said he needed a quiet place to write a paper on economics for the government. The only odd thing was they never bothered to look upstairs. Once he'd seen the basement, the 'government economist' declared: "It's perfect. We'll take it."

On Sunday 29 July, scarcely more than six weeks after Reza first encountered the BBC, Project Sam was put into operation. Joe Hunt, together with Reza, Ben and Jim Graham, stayed overnight at the Villa Motel in Belmont near Eslaminia's apartment on the San Francisco peninsula. Dean Karny put down six weeks' rent in advance on the house on Beverly Glen, and then joined the group in Belmont at around 3 p.m. the next day.

They started out for Eslaminia's apartment building, with Jim and Reza in one of the BBC's imported BMWs and the three 'shadings' in a yellow camper-van borrowed from Joe Hunt's father. In the back of the van was a large trunk, wrapped in brown paper and addressed to Hedayat Eslaminia.

To begin with all went according to plan. Joe and Ben, disguised in brown delivery uniforms, carried the trunk to Eslaminia's door with Jim Graham in close attendance. The Iranian let them in. Then things started to go wrong.

Bungled murder

Graham spilled the chloroform they'd brought for Eslaminia, and began to feel faint himself. Ben Dosti, apparently suffering from an attack of guilt, rushed into the bathroom during the struggle that followed and began furiously to wash his hands. But finally Dean and Reza, waiting in the vehicles outside, saw the other three re-emerge. This time the trunk they were carrying was obviously very heavy.

They drove for 10 minutes, then changed vehicles. As the trunk was being

Left: This is Hunt's plan for the killing of Ron Levin – called 'the recipe for murder' by the prosecution. Forensic experts found Hunt's fingerprints on the document.

Drug-peddling politician

Aged 56 when he died, an ex-member of the Shah of Iran's government and a refugee from Ayatollah Khomeini's 1978 revolution, Hedayat Eslaminia had a long history of opium addiction and brutality to his wife and children. He settled in the exclusive Hillsborough area of the San Francisco Peninsula in 1978 with his mistress and four children, while Reza's mother, Mina, lived in a house in Beverly Hills.

Violent relationship

Frequent screaming rows with his eldest child, Reza, often ended in violence. In 1979 Reza, who had already experimented with marijuana, cocaine and LSD, went into drug rehabilitation after attempting suicide by drinking drain-cleaning fluid. The highly disturbed boy swung between blaming his father and his mother for the mess he was making of his life, and in 1980 Reza's psychiatrist warned Hedayat that he could be in danger from his son. In the same year Reza was arrested three times for possession of dangerous weapons, drugs and burglary. He narrowly avoided prison.

Easy money

By 1984 Reza was 23 and in his first job, selling industrial flooring on the telephone. He hated the work and was desperate for an easy way to make big money. At the time when he met the manipulative Joe Hunt, Reza Eslaminia was in many ways a loaded gun just waiting for someone to pull the trigger.

Above: After he seized power, Ayatollah Khomeini sent secret agents to track down the Shah's officials who had escaped to exile. As a former cabinet minister, Hedayat Eslaminia was on the death list.

Right: Drug-user Eslaminia brutalised his wife and children and his eldest son Reza hated him.

Karny testifies

Dean Karny took part in the killing of Hedayat Eslaminia. Knowing he faced the death penalty if convicted, he did a deal: in return for immunity from prosecution he testified against Joe Hunt. His evidence helped secure a life sentence for the Billionaire Boys' leader. Afterwards he vanished, given a new identity under the Federal witness protection scheme.

▶ carried to a hired truck, they heard piteous cries coming from within.

"Please, sir," Eslaminia was begging, "let me out." His pleas were ignored.

Reza then drove off happily in the BMW to keep a dinner date with his girlfriend in San Francisco, while the others headed south for Los Angeles. Ben and Dean were in the back of the truck, keeping an eye on the trunk. Jim Graham drove. Joe followed in the camper.

After a while Eslaminia's cries subsided, and Ben and Dean began to worry. Joe had given them Graham's silenced Beretta and more chloroform to deal with their captive, but they were too scared to open the trunk, so they made air holes in it with a screwdriver. Soon they could hear Eslaminia gasping for air again.

Gasping for air

As the truck drove south on Interstate 5, they alternately taped over the holes when the Iranian's cries got too loud, and untaped them, when they feared he might be suffocating. It was a torture the unfortunate man would not survive.

From the camper Joe Hunt spotted that the truck's rear lights weren't working so, fearing the police might stop them, they transferred the trunk once more to the camper. Now Dean and Joe rode in the front of the camper with their victim in the back. The two boys talked happily for a time, then they noticed there had been no sound from the trunk for quite a while.

Dean took a look inside. As he lifted the lid he was greeted by a great wave of heat and a terrible stench of urine. His flashlight picked out dribble coming from the corner of the handcuffed Eslaminia's mouth. His stomach was heaving. To Dean it looked as though he was still breathing at least.

They drove on. No sound came from the trunk. Dean took another look. No movement. He checked the pulse. Nothing.

"See about giving him mouth-to-mouth

1 R
fath
the

5 The killers d
trunk into the c

Tricked by his evil son, Hedayat Eslaminia was Joe Hunt's second victim. The plan was to torture him until he revealed where he kept the money he had got out of Iran.

resuscitation," said Joe.

"He's dead, Joe," said Dean. "It's not going to do any good."

"Oh, shit," was Joe Hunt's throw-away comment. "I guess we blew it."

Back at the rented house in Los Angeles they stripped the dead man of all identifying items. Then Joe and Dean drove the body up to Soledad Canyon and dumped it down a hillside. His plan had gone wrong, but Joe Hunt was already thinking of another way to get his hands on Eslaminia's millions.

When Eslaminia's girlfriend, Olga Vasquez, reported the Iranian missing, the police immediately jumped to the conclusion that Joe Hunt had predicted. Eslaminia was a known drug-user and suspected dealer. Possibly his disappearance was drug-related, or it could be the work of Khomeini supporters. But Olga herself had her doubts about Reza. She knew about his long-standing feud with his father.

Police conclusion

When Reza visited her with Joe, looking for business documents, she asked for a policeman to be present. Then Reza made a slip.

"You know my father loved you very

Loyal girlfriend gives alibi

Joe Hunt needed an alibi for the night of Ron Levin's murder. His girlfriend, Brooke Roberts testified in court on his behalf.

On the night of 6 June, Brooke testified that she had gone to see the movie *Streets of Fire* with Dean Karny. When she got home at 9.45 p.m., she found Joe dressed for bed and brushing his teeth. He had told her he'd been over to Ron Levin's house, and got the cheque for $1.5m for rights to the rock-crushing machine.

Crucial timing

The time was important. The defence contention was that Joe couldn't have had time to murder Levin, drive the body out to Soledad Canyon, and return by 9.45 p.m. Brooke said she'd then called her mother at 10.30 p.m., and told her about the cheque.

Sole alibi

Unfortunately, when it came time for Mrs Roberts to testify, though she confirmed the telephone conversation, she admitted she hadn't herself remembered the date on which it occurred. It was Brooke who had told her mother it was 6 June.

So Joe Hunt's alibi rested solely on the

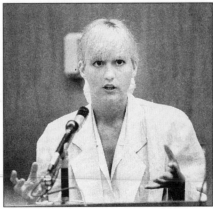

Brooke Roberts testified that Hunt was at home at the time Ron Levin was murdered.

word of his blonde girlfriend, but the jury decided that they didn't believe her. Maybe they were swayed by prosecutor Fred Wapner's question: "What is your current profession, Miss Roberts?"

"Actress," came the reply.

Suffocated in a trunk

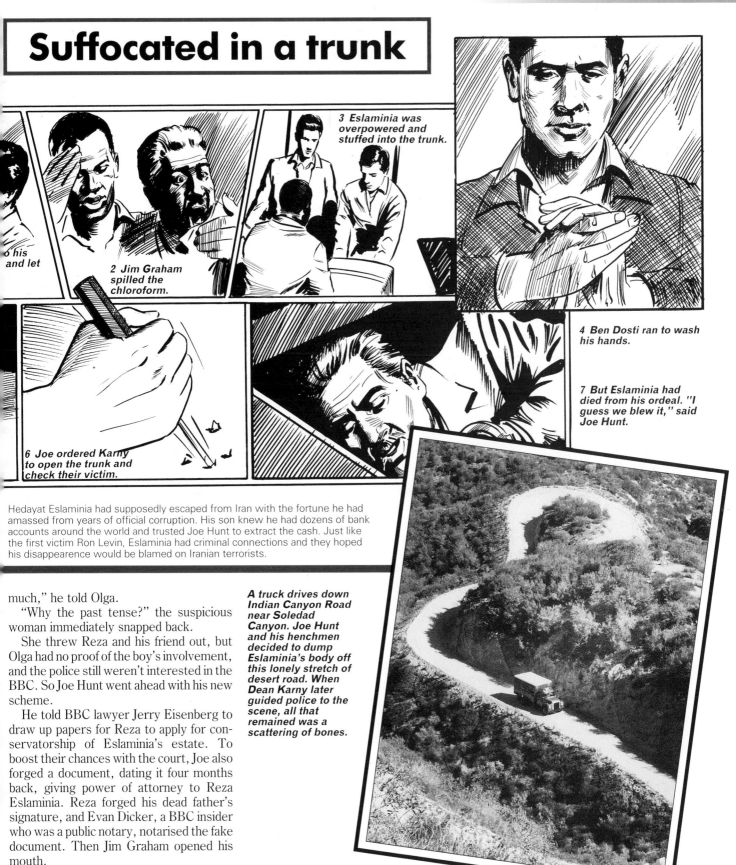

2 Jim Graham spilled the chloroform.

3 Eslaminia was overpowered and stuffed into the trunk.

o his and let

6 Joe ordered Karny to open the trunk and check their victim.

4 Ben Dosti ran to wash his hands.

7 But Eslaminia had died from his ordeal. "I guess we blew it," said Joe Hunt.

Hedayat Eslaminia had supposedly escaped from Iran with the fortune he had amassed from years of official corruption. His son knew he had dozens of bank accounts around the world and trusted Joe Hunt to extract the cash. Just like the first victim Ron Levin, Eslaminia had criminal connections and they hoped his disappearence would be blamed on Iranian terrorists.

A truck drives down Indian Canyon Road near Soledad Canyon. Joe Hunt and his henchmen decided to dump Eslaminia's body off this lonely stretch of desert road. When Dean Karny later guided police to the scene, all that remained was a scattering of bones.

much," he told Olga.

"Why the past tense?" the suspicious woman immediately snapped back.

She threw Reza and his friend out, but Olga had no proof of the boy's involvement, and the police still weren't interested in the BBC. So Joe Hunt went ahead with his new scheme.

He told BBC lawyer Jerry Eisenberg to draw up papers for Reza to apply for conservatorship of Eslaminia's estate. To boost their chances with the court, Joe also forged a document, dating it four months back, giving power of attorney to Reza Eslaminia. Reza forged his dead father's signature, and Evan Dicker, a BBC insider who was a public notary, notarised the fake document. Then Jim Graham opened his mouth.

Died under torture

One night at the BBC offices Graham boasted to Jerry Eisenberg that they'd kidnapped Eslaminia and that he'd died under torture. The lawyer was appalled. He contacted the FBI. Joe Hunt's empire was starting to unravel.

On 9 August Eisenberg, along with both May twins, Jeff Raymond and two other Billionaire Boys, met FBI agents and detectives from the Beverly Hills Police Department. Evidence was mounting against Joe Hunt, but the police told Eisenberg to carry on working for the BBC to see what else he could find out.

On 16 August Reza got his conservatorship, but once again Joe Hunt's murderous plans were to go astray. The boys searched all Eslaminia's bank accounts, but

there was no sign of the promised millions. Reza thought the money must be in Switzerland, so, armed with their legal authority, Reza and Ben Dosti flew out to Zurich to continue the search.

But, meanwhile, on the very day the conservatorship was granted, the police had finally decided to take a closer look at

21

Slip of the tongue

Police initially believed that Hedayat Eslaminia had been abducted for political reasons. Reza called on his father's girlfriend to go through his belongings, looking for the details of Hedayat's bank accounts. While talking to the girlfriend, Reza made a slip of the tongue: "My father loved you very much," he said. "Why the past tense?" she replied. Reza became flustered and changed the subject.

▶ Ron Levin's apartment. After a thorough search, Les Zoeller of the Beverly Hills Police Department had come up with nothing, when Levin's stepfather, who was there to let the police in, presented him with a folder of documents. He'd found them in the apartment after Ron's disappearance.

Zoeller leafed through the papers. They looked like business documents connected with a transaction – in fact they were the fake ones that Joe had planted. Then Zoeller found something a good deal more interesting. Among the documents were seven sheets of yellow legal paper headed 'AT LEVIN'S: TO DO'. With all his elaborate planning Joe Hunt had made a simple but fatal blunder: he'd left his murder plan at the scene of the crime.

The list contained items like: 'TAPE MOUTH, HANDCUFF and KILL DOG'. Zoeller took it away for forensic testing, and the fingerprint department lifted a clear set of prints from the paper.

Joe Hunt and Jim Graham were arrested on 28 September. Hunt was fingerprinted and a match was found with the prints on the murder list. But the police weren't so confident of their case against Graham, so both men were released within a matter of days. More evidence was needed for a charge of murder to stick.

Joe was cock-a-hoop. It seemed he'd beaten the system. Reza and Ben reported things going well in Switzerland. Soon they hoped to have their hands on the money. Then Oscar Breiling of the Special Prosecutions Unit finally cracked the case wide open.

Forged letter

The forged letter from Hedayat Eslaminia giving his son power of attorney was dated 11 April 1984. One of the Swiss bankers called a friend in Los Angeles to check on the document. The friend called Breiling. Breiling then established, by checking with immigration officials, that Eslaminia had in fact been in Mexico with Olga Vasquez on 11 April. He couldn't have been in Los Angeles signing any documents on that date. The power of attorney was obviously faked.

Joe Hunt and Jim Graham found themselves back in jail on 22 October. Ben and Reza returned to the States, and then went on the run. They were not finally picked up until August of the following year. But in the meantime the police had got what they really needed to get convictions for murder against all the suspects – all but one. Dean Karny, Joe Hunt's most slavish follower,

Trial by TV

By the time the Ron Levin murder came to trial the case had received nationwide publicity in the US, and Joe Hunt was a celebrity. Increasingly he seemed to enjoy his fame, and eventually elected to act as his own lawyer in the second trial for the murder of Hedayat Eslaminia, so as to gain maximum press attention.

Mini-series

With the trials still in progress in November 1987 American TV company NBC screened a mini-series on the killings with Judd Nelson starring as Hunt. Most names were changed, but Hunt and Karny were both given their real names, and many people believed that the TV programme, which left little doubt about Hunt's and other Billionaire Boys' guilt, could be prejudicial to a fair trial. But Judge Laurence Rittenband, the flamboyant 81-year-old judge, threw out motions for a mistrial.

The May twins and fellow BBC insider Evan Dicker all assisted in making the series. Joe Hunt, on the other hand, attempted unsuccessfully to sue the TV company from prison for $7m for slander and invasion of privacy.

In December 1987 Hunt got his right of reply, when he gave a TV interview from prison himself. Rambling and sometimes incoherent, he attempted to justify himself. The "recipe for murder", he claimed, had been made simply to scare Levin, who had engineered his own disappearance. Similarly, Eslaminia had asked the BBC to help him disappear to avoid Khomeini's agents. His death, Hunt claimed, had been nothing more than a tragic accident.

Evan Dicker (above) and Tom May (right) helped television to make a mini-series on the murders. Hunt claimed this made a fair trial impossible.

had decided to save his own skin. He agreed to testify in return for full immunity. He also agreed to show the police where Eslaminia's body had been dumped.

Coyotes at work

Dean took them straight to Indian Canyon Road in the wild country around Soledad Canyon, and pointed down the slope. But the coyotes had been at work on Hedayat Eslaminia. At first only small fragments of bone and a piece of ribcage could be found, as well as fragments of hair. Then a full search uncovered what the police had been looking for – a jawbone. A comparison with Eslaminia's dental records proved that they had indeed found what remained of the Iranian ex-government minister.

With Dean Karny telling his story on the stand, the prosecution was able to get convictions against all the defendants. Joe Hunt himself was found guilty of first-degree murder and sentenced to life imprisonment without possibility of parole. The roller-coaster ride from Chicago poverty to the high life of Los Angeles yuppie ended for the founder of the Billionaire Boys' Club in Folsom Prison.

Evil Mind

Killer Yuppie

Joe Hunt was born Joseph Henry Gamsky in Chicago on Hallowe'en 1959. His father, Larry Gamsky, a cold and dictatorial character, had his own strange ideas about how to bring up children. He forbade Joe and his brother and sister from calling him Dad, saying: "I want you to think of me as your teacher, not your father." He wouldn't let his wife Kathy walk young Joe to kindergarten school for fear of spoiling him. Always in financial trouble, Larry even confiscated the money eight-year-old Joe earned from his paper round.

Constant battle

Life in the Gamsky household was a constant battle. When Larry and Kathy Gamsky finally divorced during Joe's last year at school, the other two children sided with their mother. But Joe, despite his harsh treatment as a child, chose to live with the tyrannical and manipulative Larry. Before long he would become a carbon copy of his father.

It was Gamsky Senior who pushed Joe through his accountancy exams at just 19 years old. Later Joe would say his father had "hypnotised him for success". Then Larry decided to change his name to something, as he put it, "less ethnic-sounding", becoming Ryan Hunt. So Joe followed suit: in 1981 Joe Gamsky became Joe Hunt.

Ruthless drive

Much of Joe Hunt's ruthless drive for success seems to have come from a desperate desire to please his cold and distant father. In the same way, the weak young men who surrounded Joe in the Billionaire Boys' Club were just as desperate to please him. On one occasion when Joe was arrested for a traffic offence, the police station was besieged by Billionaire Boys competing to pay his $100 fine.

Joe encouraged his followers to band ever more closely together, living in groups in the luxury condominiums of Los Angeles. He taught them to call outsiders by the derisive name of 'normies'. He used Paradox Philosophy, essentially no more than a rationale for ruthless selfishness, to

Then called Joe Gamsky, Hunt won a scholarship to Harvard Prep School. He was clever, ambitious and utterly ruthless.

undermine their every decent feeling.

As Joe described his philosophy himself: "It's a bit like turning black into white." Thus his suspension from the Chicago Mercantile Exchange was made to look like the jealous reaction of petty bureaucrats to the brilliant Joe Hunt, and the murder of Ron Levin was presented to the group simply as an unavoidable business necessity.

Yuppie family

With their BMWs and their fancy apartments, coupled with Joe Hunt's warped philosophy of life and their hero-worship of him, the Boys of the BBC who became embroiled in the murders of Levin and Eslaminia were a yuppified 1980s version of Charles Manson's 'Family'. Like Manson, at whose instructions the horrific Tate-LaBianca murders were carried out, Joe Hunt had the power to make some of his followers break the ultimate taboo simply on his say-so.

Hunt's brief career in Chicago ended in disaster when he was caught cheating on the commodities market. Inset: Hunt, in prison uniform after being convicted of killing Levin, faces his second murder trial.

GRAHAM YOUNG

The Teacup POISONER

Right: Graham Young was that rare modern criminal – the homicidal poisoner. He had been sent to Broadmoor, the hospital for the criminally insane, at the age of 14.

Poisoners are a rare breed. They generally make their cold, premeditated, drawn-out attacks on friends and family. Graham Young was one such evil killer.

Poison – that favourite weapon of the Victorian murderer – is a comparative rarity nowadays. It accounts for less than three per cent of all criminal homicides in the developed world. Modern science and the fact that the poisoner is usually closely related to his victim makes for ease of detection.

There remains, however, the rare but real spectre of a motiveless, psychopathic poisoner with means and opportunity . . .

In the spring of 1971, 23-year-old Graham Young applied for a job at the John Hadland Laboratories, manufacturers of photographic equipment, at Bovington, Hertfordshire. A neat, precisely spoken young man, he told the managing director, Godfrey Foster, that he had not worked since leaving school because of a nervous breakdown, but was now fully recovered. Foster was impressed and took Young on as an assistant storeman.

Young's immediate boss at Hadland was 60-year-old Bob Egle, the head storeman. By pure chance an outbreak of gastro-enteritis, so severe that it had become known as the 'Bovington Bug', had been sweeping the local community, and when Bob Egle fell ill a couple of months after Young's arrival it seemed that he had caught it.

Unfortunately the normally fit and active storeman became

The tea lady at Hadland's delivered refreshments to the hatch behind which the storemen worked. Young always collected the tea for his workmates, taking the opportunity to add his deadly poisons to the cups.

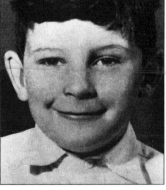

Above: Graham Young was a quiet child, but he developed a precocious interest in black magic, Nazism and poisons.

much more sick than was characteristic of 'The Bug'; he suffered violent vomiting, severe pains in his chest and back, loss of balance and, eventually, wild delirium. He was taken to the intensive care unit at St Alban's City Hospital, where he died on 19 July.

Godfrey Foster attended Bob Egle's funeral, and took Graham Young with him as representative of Bob's workmates. On the way they spoke of Egle's disease, and Foster was impressed by Young's seemingly wide knowledge of medical matters.

A nice cup of tea

Bob Egle's replacement as head storeman was 56-year-old Fred Biggs. Towards the end of October, by what appeared to be appalling bad luck, Biggs, too, fell ill. After two days off work he struggled in on Saturday, 30 October, and his assistant Graham Young greeted him with a nice cup of tea. By Monday, Biggs was desperately sick with the same symptoms as Egle; he was taken to the National Hospital for Nervous Diseases, London, where he died on 19 November.

Throughout the winter, other Hadland employees suffered similar symptoms. Two of them, Jethro Batt and David Tilson, were seriously ill. Fearing that the leakage of chemicals used at Hadland's was responsible for the tragedies that had hit the formerly happy company, Godfrey Foster called in a team of consultant toxicologists, headed by Dr Iain Anderson.

To reassure the staff, Dr Anderson held a meeting and invited questions. The first questioner was Graham Young, who wanted to know if the doctor didn't think the symptoms of Egle, Biggs, Batt and Tilson bore all the signs of thallium poisoning?

Dr Anderson was intrigued. Thallium, a relatively rare compound, was used at the factory in the manufacture of camera lenses, but its history as a homicide poison was sparse. On checking, Dr Anderson found that many of the victims' symptoms – numbness in arms and legs, chest pains, loss of hair and delirium – could be equated with thallium poisoning. But how did this young storeman know about it? With his suspicions aroused, Dr Anderson asked Scotland Yard to check for any record of Graham Young. The Yard's records shocked the John Hadland employees and even startled Dr Anderson.

In 1962, at the age of 14, Graham Young had been convicted of murdering his stepmother by poison and attempting to poison his father, sister and a school friend. He had been committed to Broadmoor, the institution for the criminally insane, but had been pronounced cured in 1971 and released.

During his nine years in custody, Young had read every book on chemicals and medicine that the prison library could provide; no-one in authority seems to have noticed the connection between his crime and his 'inside' interest. In any case, when he came out and was hired by Hadland's, Young had no difficulty in spotting the potential of the laboratory's supply of thallium.

Until the 1940s, thallium salts had had a limited medical use as a treatment for ringworm and facial hair in women, but were abandoned because of the discomfort a dose of even two grains could cause.

Fatal dose

Twelve grains was the fatal dose, and Young had used slightly more than that to kill Bob Egle and Fred Biggs. He laced their tea with the poison over a period of time, and revelled in their increasing agony. Despite the fact that Egle had been cremated, an analysis of his ashes, which had been buried in an urn, showed a remaining nine milligrams of thallium, the residue of a huge dose.

Young was arrested, and police found a grim but metic- ➤

Above and right: In his early 20s Graham Young convinced the authorities that he was a reformed character. Released from Broadmoor despite the protests of some of the hospital's nursing staff, Young was given a medical certificate stating that he was fully cured.

Left: Suspected of killing his stepmother, whose body had been cremated, 14-year-old Graham Young was tried at the Old Bailey for the attempted murder of his father, sister and a friend.

Department of Employment and Productivity
Government Training Centre
119–122 Buckingham Avenue Slough Bucks

Telephone 23326

Your reference

Mr Foster
Messrs John Hadland (Photo
Instrumentation) Ltd
New House Laboratories
New House Road
BOVINGTON, Herts.

Our reference

Date 26 April 1971

Dear Sir

In response to your request I am forwarding a copy of Dr Unwin's report on Mr Young. I am sure you will find this satisfactory.

Yours faithfully

J R AYLES

JRA/EJ

COPY

15 January 1971

Medical Certificate
Graham Frederick YOUNG

This man has suffered a deep going personality disorder which necessitated his hospitalization throughout the whole of his adolescence. He has, however, made an extremely full recovery and is now entirely fit for discharge, his sole disability now being the need to catch up on his lost time.

He is capable of undertaking any sort of work without any restrictions as to residence, travel or environment. His natural bent is towards the non-manual and clerical and in the first instance he would do extremely well training as a store keeper. He is of above average intelligence and capable of sustained effort. He would fit in well and not draw any attention to himself in any community.

(E.L Unwin)
Consultant Psychiatrist

ss poisoner found guilty .. now the sensational revelation

HE'S DONE IT
BEFORE

Released from Broadmoor only 16 months ago

Evening News Reporters

GRAHAM YOUNG was jailed for life day for murdering two workmates

THE VICTIMS

Schoolboy Aged 14 Goes To Broadmoor

HE POISONED FAMILY FOOD –JUDGE TOLD

A 14-YEAR-OLD Crickle-wood secondary nother who put poison

From the Evening J

Serious error to POIS
free him

ulous diary detailing the doses of thallium he had given to each of his victims. The dapper assistant storeman appeared to have been conducting a macabre experiment in death, measuring the time between dosage and first discomfort. Apart from Egle, Biggs, Batt and Tilson, Young had given the poison to at least four other people who had escaped relatively unscathed.

In June 1972 Graham Young was charged at St Alban's Crown Court on two counts of murder, two of attempted murder and four of malicious poisoning, and was sentenced to life imprisonment.

Police had found and confiscated a packet of thallium – "My exit dose," Young called it – in the lining of his jacket. He had told his warders at the trial that if he was convicted, he would "break his own neck" on the dock rail. In fact, Graham Young survived for another 18 years in Parkhurst Prison, dying there of a heart attack in August 1990.

Above: The Graham Young case was a press sensation, especially when it was discovered that he had poisoned before.

Young's two fatal victims at Hadland's were Fred Biggs (left) and Bob Egle (below). Both were helpful to their new colleague, but both were repaid with long, agonising suffering that ended in death.

Graham Young's release from Broadmoor after only nine years was a bureaucratic decision, carried out against the advice of many of the nursing staff. The nurses' fears were to prove tragically well-founded.

CHARLES MANSON

"DEATH TO PIGS"

Actress Sharon Tate was eight months pregnant when she became the most famous victim of Charles Manson's drug-crazed followers.

Manson was a hardened criminal, who at 32 had already spent 17 years in jail before he was released to travel to California. Inset: Twenty-six-year-old Sharon Tate and her friends were victims chosen at random.

At 8.30 a.m. on 9 August 1969 a middle-aged black woman pounded on the front door of 10090 Cielo Drive in the hills above Los Angeles' exclusive Bel Air district. The woman was Winifred Chapman, housekeeper two doors down at the rented home of film director Roman Polanski and his pregnant wife, actress Sharon Tate. Mrs Chapman was screaming hysterically: "Murder, death, bodies, blood!"

Householder Ray Asin came to the door, and his 15-year-old son, Jim, made the call to the Los Angeles Police Department (LAPD), and thus revealed to the world what the state's prosecutor would later call: "The most bizarre, savage, nightmarish murder in the recorded annals of crime."

Bodies on the lawn

When the police arrived at 10050 Cielo Drive, a substantial mansion set in its own grounds, they found a scene of appalling carnage. In a car parked in the driveway was the bloody body of a young man slumped over the wheel. He had been shot four times. On the lawn were the bodies of a man in his 30s and a young, dark-haired woman in a nightgown. The man had been shot twice, struck over the head 13 times and stabbed a total of 51 times. The woman had 28 stab wounds. Both were soaked in their own blood.

Fearing the killer might still be around,

27

SHARON TATES FATHER WAS A BRITISH AIR FORCE PILOT (EX)

POLICE CASEBOOK

police entered the house through a back window. In the living room they found two more bodies. A young, blonde woman, dressed only in a flowered bra and panties, was lying in a foetal position in front of the fireplace. She was heavily pregnant. She was also soaked in blood. A white nylon rope had been looped around her neck, over a rafter and then around the neck of a man who lay four feet away. He had a bloody towel over his face and his hands were still raised, as if protecting his head. He had been stabbed seven times and shot once.

The pregnant woman had a total of 16 stab wounds, five of which would have been fatal on their own. On the lower part

of the front door the word PIG had been roughly printed in what tests would later prove was her blood. The woman was Sharon Tate.

Before they even knew who the victims were, the police had a suspect. Approaching the guesthouse on the other side of the swimming pool they heard a dog barking and a man's voice saying: "Shh, be quiet."

Police burst in and found 19-year-old William Garretson. He was the caretaker, hired by owner Rudi Altobelli to look after the guesthouse, while the main house was let. Garretson said he'd been there all night, and had heard nothing suspicious. When police took him on a tour of the house to show him the mayhem he'd failed to ▶

Death of a star

Roman Polanski met Sharon Tate in 1966 in London during the filming of his spoof horror film, *The Fearless Vampire Killers*. He was already a star director after *Repulsion* and *Cul de Sac*. Nevertheless, critics, who praised his films, commented on his apparent obsession with violence and satanism. It was the box-office success of his next film, *Rosemary's Baby*, in 1967 that really made Hollywood sit up and take notice.

Overdose

Despite her beauty, Sharon Tate's movie career never really got out of first gear. Her best part was as Jennifer, the actress in *The Valley of the Dolls*, who takes an overdose of sleeping tablets.

Friends said that at the time of her death Sharon was simply looking forward to being a mother. She had come back from Europe early, while her husband, Polanski, finished work on a film.

Roman Polanski and Sharon Tate had been married for just 18 months when 'Crazy Sadie' killed her and her unborn child.

Bel Air Massacre

This was the scene in the living room where Sharon Tate and Jay Sebring were killed.

The Deputy DA shows a picture of the nylon rope used to tie up Sharon Tate and Jay Sebring.

Number 10050 Cielo Drive lies at the end of an exclusive cul-de-sac off Benedict Canyon Road, Bel Air. This secluded luxury bungalow was rented by Roman Polanksi and his wife Sharon Tate. Polanski was in England completing a film when Manson's followers attacked; Sharon had returned early as she was expecting a baby in a few weeks. While the Polanskis were away their friends Abigail Folger and Voytek Frykowski had stayed in the house, and they were still there when the killers struck. Another friend, Jay Sebring, had the fatal misfortune to be visiting the house that night. The fifth victim was 18-year-old Steven Parent. He had come to visit the caretaker, who lived in the guesthouse situated on the other side of the swimming pool. The caretaker – the only living person found at Cielo Drive that morning by police – was immediately arrested, but he was released within 24 hours.

SHARON TATE begged Sadie (Susan Atkins) for her life, saying she wanted to have her baby. Sadie later said that her only regret was not having time to slice open Sharon's womb and cut out the eyes of the other victims.

JAY SEBRING was known to like tying women up before sex and former girlfriends admitted they had been whipped by him. Some papers suggested that the murders had resulted from a sado-masochistic orgy.

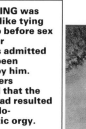

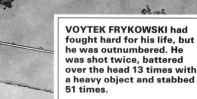

ABIGAIL FOLGER was found barefoot, wearing nothing but a white nightdress, saturated with blood. She had made a run for it, but Katie (Patricia Krenwinkel) caught her and knocked her to the ground. She then stabbed her 28 times.

VOYTEK FRYKOWSKI had fought hard for his life, but he was outnumbered. He was shot twice, battered over the head 13 times with a heavy object and stabbed 51 times.

Bloodstains were found inside and outside the house. In addition to the word 'PIG' daubed on the door in Sharon Tate's blood, the killers had walked around the building with blood dripping from their clothes. They also left their fingerprints all over the house.

Among the mourners at Sharon Tate's funeral were Kirk Douglas, Warren Beatty, Steve McQueen, James Coburn, Yul Brynner, Peter Sellers and John and Michelle Phillips of The Mamas and the Papas.

Hairdresser to the stars

Many of the same stars turned out for Jay Sebring's funeral as well. He was well known as a hairdresser to the stars, but also had a reputation as a heavy drug-taker with a liking for tying women up and whipping them before making love. He and Sharon had been lovers before she met Polanski.

Statutory rape

Within a few years Polanski went on to get into trouble with the law himself on a charge of statutory rape. He skipped bail, fled to Europe, and has never been able to return to the US.

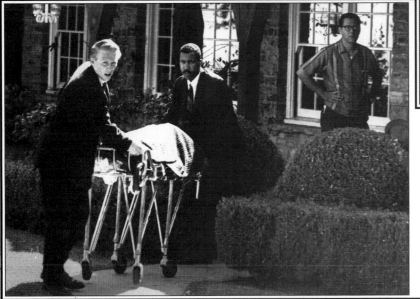

Top: Beautiful Sharon Tate was stabbed 16 times.

Inset: Manson told his followers to kill wealthy white families in such a way that the murders would be blamed on black people – thus igniting a race war.

Left: Sharon Tate's body is wheeled out of the house.

▶ hear, he was unable to identify any of the bodies. Dissatisfied with his story, the police placed Garretson under arrest, but within 24 hours they were forced to release him after he passed a polygraph test.

The LAPD were left with the bloodiest of jigsaw puzzles. By now the bodies had been identified. The man in the living room roped to Sharon Tate was Jay Sebring, 35, an internationally known hairdresser. The couple on the lawn were Voytek Frykowski, 32, Polish-born playboy and friend of Roman Polanski, and Abigail Folger, 25, his girlfriend and heiress to the Folger coffee fortune. The young man in the car was Steven Earl Parent, 18, a delivery boy, who'd visited Garretson that night to try to sell him a clock radio. What was missing was a motive for their slaughter.

Ritual slaying

The press were screaming "ritual slaying", after someone got hold of the incorrect idea that the bodies had been found with hoods over their heads. They also highlighted the fact that Sharon was found only partially clothed, and that Sebring was her ex-lover. There were suggestions of a sex orgy that had ended in death.

But the police were looking for more solid motives. Robbery seemed unlikely. There were money and valuables lying around the house in plain view. None of the victims had been sexually assaulted. But drugs including marijuana, hashish, cocaine and the hallucinogenic MDA were found, and autopsy reports later revealed MDA in the systems of both Folger and Frykowski. So the police theorised at this early stage either a drug party "freak-out" in which someone had gone crazy and killed, or a drug deal gone wrong. They also entertained the possibility of "deaths by hire". But there were flaws in all these theories.

Outside the property the phone wires had been carefully cut. If it was a drug freak-out, this could only have been done after the murders, which made no sense at all. Also, how could one person possibly have wreaked so much carnage? On the other hand the very savagery of the attacks told against the idea of a professional killing, so the police were left with a drug burn. In fact, so convinced were they that this was the result of an argument over drugs or money or both, that they totally ignored one lead that could have led them to a solution to the case within days.

The Los Angeles Sheriff's Office (LASO), working quite separately from the LAPD, had arrested a hippie musician called Bobby Beausoleil on 6 August for the murder of music teacher Gary Hinman. Hinman had been brutally stabbed to death but, more significantly, the words POLITICAL PIGGY had been written in blood on the wall in his home. Beausoleil had been caught driving Hinman's Fiat with the murder weapon still in the car.

The LASO told the LAPD that their suspect lived with a bunch of other hippies on Spahn Ranch, an old movie location in the Simi Hills outside the LA suburb of Chatsworth. Their leader, whom they seemed to believe was Jesus Christ, was a man called Charlie.

But Sergeant Jess Buckles, assigned to the Tate killings, wasn't interested. "We know what's behind these murders," he told LASO detectives. "They're part of a big dope transaction."

Horrific killings

That same night the LAPD would have another horrendous double murder on their hands. But even the seemingly glaring similarities to the Tate killings wouldn't be acknowledged for three months.

At 8.30 p.m. on Sunday 10 August, the day after the discovery of the five bodies on Cielo Drive, 15-year-old Frank Struthers returned from a boating trip to his home at 3301 Waverly Drive near Griffith Park. There appeared to be no-one home, though the blinds were down and his mother and stepfather, Rosemary and Leno LaBianca, should have been in. He called his sister, Susan, and together with her boyfriend, Joe Dorgan, they found a spare key and entered the house.

Leno LaBianca was lying on his back on the living room floor in his pyjamas with a bloody pillow-case over his head. Around

Manson's Family of crazed followers

Charles Manson   Patricia Krenwinkel   Charles 'Tex' Watson   Susan Atkins   Leslie van Houten

Patricia Krenwinkel, alias Katie, was one of Manson's most devoted followers. She chased after Abigail Folger after the young heiress had escaped from her bonds and tried to run for help. Catching her on the lawn, Katie stabbed her 28 times. A psychiatrist's report said that Katie had little grip on reality and might lapse into total psychosis if separated from the group. Charles 'Tex' Watson led the attack on Sharon Tate and her friends. He shot Steven Parent and Jay Sebring and helped kill the women too. He has spent the last 24 years in jail and is trying to secure his parole. Susan Atkins, alias Sadie, stabbed Sharon Tate to death as the young actress pleaded for mercy. It was Sadie boasting about the murders after her arrest that helped solve the case. Leslie van Houten was the least devoted of the Manson girls, but she killed for him, helping Katie stab Rosemary LaBianca to death. State prosecutor Vincent Bugliosi has stated that van Houten's years in jail have hardened her further and he has little hope of her eventual rehabilitation.

his neck was the flex from a heavy lamp, tied tightly enough to have strangled him. His hands were tied behind him with a leather thong. He had been stabbed repeatedly in the abdomen with a knife, and from his stomach an ivory-handled carving fork still projected. Carved in his flesh was the word WAR.

When the police arrived they found Rosemary LaBianca in the bedroom. She was lying in a pool of blood, her short pink nightgown and a dress she appeared to have put on over it both bunched above her head. Like her husband she had a pillowcase over her head and a lamp flex tied tightly round her neck. She had been stabbed 41 times in the back and legs.

In the living room high on one wall was written in blood the words DEATH TO PIGS. On the opposite wall by the front door was the word RISE. And on the door of the refrigerator in the kitchen, also in blood, someone had written HEALTER SKELTER (sic).

But almost immediately police rejected the idea that the same killers might be behind the Tate and LaBianca murders. If anything they thought the LaBiancas might be a copycat. When it was found that Leno, president of a chain of LA supermarkets, had gambling debts they started to work on the theory that it could have been a Mafia hit. And still no-one was interested in connecting either case to the Hinman killing.

That Saturday the police did raid Spahn Ranch, but they weren't looking for murderers, they were running down an auto-theft gang, who'd been stealing VWs and converting them into dune buggies. The raid was not a success. All 26 suspects had to be released when it was found that warrants had been misdated. Among those arrested, and then released, was a 34-year-old ex-con-man out on parole. His name was Charles Manson.

Broken gun grip

Meanwhile, LAPD's separate investigations into the Tate and LaBianca murders were making little progress. They had 25 unidentified fingerprints inside the Tate mansion. They had three pieces of a broken gun grip also found at Cielo Drive, and these were identified as belonging to a Buntline Special Hi-Standard .22 Longhorn revolver. A description of this quite unusual weapon was circulated but no information came back. They'd also found a Buck knife down the back of a chair and a pair of spectacles. None of these clues had taken them anywhere.

Below: Manson and his hippy commune lived at the Spahn Ranch, north of Los Angeles. Police investigating car thefts raided it and arrested 26 people, including Manson.

Sandra Good (left) and Lynette 'Squeaky' Fromme (right) took part in frequent sex orgies at the Ranch.

Bones and remains at the Family's home

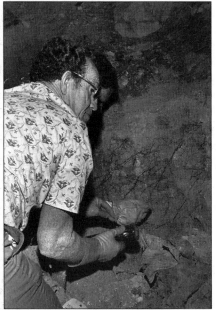

Left: Coroner's officials search for the remains of Shorty Shea. Manson killed him and had his body chopped up and buried in pieces near the commune.

Tex Watson was arrested in his home state of Texas, and fought extradition to California long and hard. He was eventually tried separately from the others, and given the same death sentence, later commuted to life imprisonment.

Manson, along with Clem (Steve Grogan) and Bruce Davis, was also given life for the murder of Shorty Shea, a horse wrangler at Spahn. Shorty was hacked to death probably on 25 or 26 August with four German bayonets and a pirate's cutlass that Manson had appropriated from the leader of the Straight Satans. His head and limbs were cut off and buried to prevent identification. The body was never found.

Though it was never proved, various members of the Family may have been responsible for at least 11 other murders. These include:

- John Philip Haught, known in the Family as Zero. On 5 November 1969 four other Family members, including Bruce Davis, reported to police that Zero had shot himself while playing Russian roulette. A verdict of suicide was recorded although the gun had contained seven bullets, not one, and no prints of any kind were found on it or its leather holster, suggesting they had been wiped.

- Joel Pugh, ex-Family member, was found dead on 2 December 1969 in the Talgarth Hotel in London. His throat and wrists were slashed. Two bloody razor blades lay nearby. On the mirror was weird reversed writing and drawings. The coroner's verdict was suicide, but a letter was found in a motel in Independence, addressed to Pugh's wife, a member of the Family, which suggested otherwise. The unidentified sender wrote: "I would not want what happened to Joel to happen to me."

- On 20 November 1970 Ronald Hughes, originally Manson's lawyer, and representing Lulu (Leslie van Houten) at the trial, failed to show up in court. He hadn't come back from his weekend camping trip. On the day of the verdict his badly decomposed body was found in a remote part of Ventura County. Cause of death could not be determined. Later, during the making of a documentary film on the Family, Sandy told director Laurence Merrick that the Family had killed "35 to 40 people" and "Hughes was the first of the retaliation murders". The lawyer had refused to go along with Manson's trial strategy to let the girls take all the blame, so Manson had had him killed.

The drug connection was making no progress either. Four drug dealers who had been frequent visitors to 10050 Cielo Drive were prime suspects for a while, but were later eliminated when three proved alibis and another passed a polygraph. As for the LaBianca detectives, they simply had no leads at all.

Fear among Hollywood luminaries who had been friends of Sharon Tate was rife, as they began to think they might be next on some maniac's list. Frank Sinatra was in hiding. Mia Farrow was too frightened to attend the funeral. Sales of guard dogs and guns for personal protection rocketed.

Then on 10 October 1969 police in Independence, a town 5½ hours north of LA, mounted a raid on the Barker Ranch in the rugged and desolate Panamint Mountains just south of Death Valley. They were investigating an arson attack and a series of car thefts, but local rumour also told stories of orgies, drug use and a crazed band of hippies called the Manson Family, who rode round the desert in dune buggies

re-enacting Rommel's battles in North Africa.

The first raid resulted in 10 women and three men being arrested. Two babies, both with severe sunburn, were also discovered. Police recovered a number of stolen vehicles and a store of arms including a sub-machine gun.

Manson arrested

Two days later the police went back and arrested seven more people. Searching the primitive bathroom at the back, one officer noticed long, dark hair hanging out of the top of a tiny cupboard under the wash basin. When challenged, a man dressed in buckskin came out, cracking a joke about the cramped space. He was booked in Independence as "Manson, Charles M. aka Jesus Christ, God".

Among the young girls picked up in the Barker raid was Kitty Lutesinger, 17, a girlfriend of Bobby Beausoleil who was already in custody for the Hinman murder.

Man with a mission

In the Haight-Ashbury district of San Francisco in the "summer of love" of 1967 the Family was born. Manson became a magnet for the lost and desperate – especially young girls. Sadie, one of the first to join the Family, described meeting him for the first time. Her experience seems to have been typical.

"I was sitting in the living-room, and a man walked in and he had a guitar with him, and all of a sudden he was surrounded by a group of girls." Manson started to sing. "I knew at the time that he was something I'd been looking for . . . and I went down and kissed his feet."

A couple of days later they had sex, during which Manson told her to imagine he was her father. "I did so," Sadie remembered, "and it was a very beautiful experience."

The Family, whose hard-core members numbered between 25 and 30 but sometimes included 100 people, were on the road for a year and a half before settling at Spahn Ranch in August 1968. They lived mostly by begging, stealing credit cards, and taking food from restaurant trash cans. Later they also got into stealing cars.

Sex orgies

For a time Manson, who believed women's only function was to service men, organised orgies at least once a week. He would hand out grass, peyote or LSD, always taking slightly less than his followers, and then dictate who would do what with whom.

By encouraging people to overcome all restraints – he called them "hang-ups" – Manson produced an atmosphere of total amorality. He told the young and impressionable people who flocked to him that there was no such thing as wrong, and they should "never ask why. Everything was good. Whatever you do is what you're supposed to do; you are following your own karma." Over and over he repeated one of his favourite phrases: "No sense makes sense." It was a philosophy that would eventually lead some of them to commit murder without question when he told them to.

Son of God

Gradually Manson's obsessions moved from drugs and sex to other things. He changed his middle name from Milles to Willis, interpreting his name now as Charles' Will Is Man's Son – in other words: his will was that of Christ. Though he never directly claimed it himself, the Family came to believe that Manson was both Christ and the Devil.

He told them the end of the world was at hand, that the blacks would rise up and kill the whites in a massive war, which he called Helter Skelter, and that the Family would then take over the world. The term "Helter Skelter" he took from the Beatles' White Album of 1968. Apparently he was unaware that in England a helter skelter is a fairground slide.

Manson was obsessed with all Beatles

Kitty was five months pregnant, frightened and asking for protection. She told police it was Manson who had sent Beausoleil along with another of his followers, whom he'd christened Sadie Mae Glutz. The plan had been to extort money from Hinman, an ex-member of the Family. But when he'd refused Bobby had stabbed him.

The police had a hard time working out

Right: Lynette Fromme was arrested for attempting to give a hamburger laced with LSD to a prosecution witness.

Far right: Manson carved a swastika in his forehead for his court appearance. Below: Seen here in Vacaville jail in 1980, after 10 years in prison, Manson is still unrepentant.

music, but especially with the White Album, which he believed was full of messages directed specifically at him, acknowledging him as the incarnation of Christ, and encouraging him to record an album which would spark off the revolution. Thus the gentle ballad *Blackbird* became a message to the blacks to rise up, and *Helter Skelter* itself became a description of the Family descending into the Bottomless Pit of Revelation and Hopi Indian legend, and then emerging to take over the world. Most chillingly, George Harrison's humorous *Piggies*, with its references to "forks and knives", produced the bloody words scrawled in the Tate and LaBianca homes during the murders.

Bottomless Pit

The cacophonous *Revolution 9* Manson associated with the ninth chapter of Revelation, the last book of the Bible. Saint John's "four angels" became the four Beatles. He drew attention to the

description: "Their faces were as the faces of men . . . (yet) . . . they had hair as the hair of women." The fifth angel, mentioned in the first verse, was Manson himself. "And the fifth angel sounded, and I saw a star fall from heaven unto earth; and to him was given the key of the Bottomless Pit." This was the civilisation under the earth, whose entrance was in Death Valley, where the Family would live during Helter Skelter.

Race war

So here was the bizarre motive for these hideous crimes – Helter Skelter. As he told one member: "I had to show blackie how to do it." Manson believed he had to set Helter Skelter going, that if he committed horrible enough crimes in the white districts of Los Angeles it would spark off a race war. By undermining their morality, feeding them drugs and mumbo jumbo, and isolating them from the normal world, Manson had by now produced a group of slavish idolaters who would do it for him.

do every day of the week," Graham would later say.

But Sadie had other, more shocking stories to tell. Soon she was informing her fellow prisoners that she had done the Tate killings as well, once again on Manson's instructions. The way Sadie told it, two other girls and a man had also been involved. Virginia Graham's question was the same one the police had asked: Why?

Merciless killers

They "wanted to do a crime that would shock the world," was Sadie's answer, "that the world would have to stand up and take notice." But that wasn't all. Charlie had told them the Family was "chosen" to go out into the world and release randomly selected people from the Earth. Sadie told Graham: "You have to have a real love in your heart to do this for people."

It was she herself who had stabbed the pregnant Sharon Tate. "It was just like going into nothing, going into air," she told Ronnie Howard. Sharon had begged for mercy, begged to be allowed to have her baby. "Look, bitch," Sadie had told her, "I don't care about you. I don't care if you're

who was whom after the Barker raid. All the girls seemed to have a bewildering range of aliases. But eventually they established that Sadie Mae Glutz was really Susan Atkins. She was booked and sent to the Sybil Brand Institute, LA's women's prison. And it was there that she began to tell her bizarre story to fellow inmates, who were soon calling her Crazy Sadie.

Sadie bragged of her sexual exploits and first degree murder charge to anyone who would listen, but most of all she talked to two ex-prostitutes, Virginia Graham and Ronnie Howard. She told them how she had in fact stabbed Hinman while Bobby held him. But it was her way of telling the tale that astonished the other women – "just like it was a perfectly natural thing to going to have a baby. You're going to die, and I don't feel anything about it." And the killing itself? "It's like a sexual release," was Sadie's description. "Especially when you see the blood spurting out. It's better than a climax."

Then Sadie started to tell the story of the next night at the LaBianca house. It was the Family who'd committed that slaughter, too, this time with Manson himself in attendance.

Normally the cons' code would have prevented Graham and Howard from snitching, but this was just too big and too horrible to keep to themselves. So, after months of fruitless investigations, LAPD detectives were suddenly handed the whole case on a plate. From conversations with the other Family girls and a couple of bikers – members of the Straight Satan gang – whom Manson had tried to recruit, they were able to piece together the whole

story of the two nights when Manson had tried to start what he called "Helter Skelter".

Manson had preached to his Family for two years that a civil war was imminent in America between blacks and whites. It was this war that he called Helter Skelter. While Helter Skelter was in progress, the Family would hide in an underground world to which there was an entrance in Death Valley. The blacks would be victorious, but when they found themselves unable to run the country, they would invite Manson and the Family to take over.

Selecting the victims

On the afternoon of Friday 8 August, Manson told a group of selected followers: "Now is the time for Helter Skelter." The war was taking too long to happen. It was up to him to get it started. The venue Man-

son had chosen was a house where record producer Terry Melcher had lived. Manson, who fancied himself as a singer and guitarist, had nursed hopes that Melcher would give him a record deal, but the main reasons for selecting the house seem to have been because it was isolated and because both Manson and his right-hand man Charles 'Tex' Watson, 23, knew the layout of the place, having been there to parties on a number of occasions.

That evening Manson gave a knife and his favourite .22 revolver to Tex, and told him to go and kill everybody in the house "as gruesome as [he] could". To help him Manson selected Sadie (Susan Atkins) and Katie (Patricia Krenwinkel), two of his hard-core followers, both just 21 years old, and Linda Kasabian, 20, a newcomer, who was the only one of the Family with a valid driver's licence. He told them all to put on dark clothes and carry knives.

Like Hitler, Manson was a strict vegetarian. There were many strange similarities between him and the Nazi leader. Manson was also short, and made up for his lack of stature with an ability to manipulate people – particulary the gormless drifters he gathered around him in California (right).

Breaking the vow of silence

Right: Manson's death sentence was commuted to life imprisonment after the California Supreme Court banned the death penalty in 1972. This brutal mass murderer is now eligible for parole.

In an attempt to recruit Straight Satan Al Springer to the Family, Manson told the biker: "Whatever happens the girls will take the rap." During the trial it became clear that this was his strategy to avoid conviction himself.

Sadie, Katie and Lulu told their defence lawyers that they wanted to take the stand, and say they had planned and committed the murders alone. Rather than go along with this the three lawyers refused to question their clients.

Love letters

Eventually Manson, who was still receiving love letters in prison from girls wanting to join the Family, himself took the stand. In the absence of the jury he made a long, rambling and sometimes incoherent statement. Essentially his line was that Tex and the girls did what they did, but it wasn't his fault.

"These children that come at you with knives, they are your children," Manson told the court. "You taught them. I didn't teach them. I just tried to help them stand up."

"Go with Tex," he told the girls, "and do whatever he tells you to do."

Apparently they assumed they were going on one of their regular "creepy crawling" missions, during which they broke into houses at night and moved things around while the occupants slept.

But as the group were about to drive away in one of the Spahn Ranch hand's '59 Ford, Manson leaned into the car and added: "Leave a sign. You girls know what to write. Something witchy." It is a measure of the extraordinary power Manson held over the Family that none of them thought to question him further.

They drove into Benedict Canyon and parked outside 10050 Cielo Drive. Tex climbed a telegraph pole outside the house and cut the phone wires. Then they left the car at the bottom of the hill and returned on foot.

The four dark-clad figures scaled the fence, and immediately saw the headlights of Steve Parent's Rambler coming down the drive. Tex told the girls to drop flat. Then he went over, called out "Halt!" and shot the driver four times.

"I am the devil"

Up at the house Tex slit a screen on one of the windows and climbed in. He opened the front door and let Sadie and Katie in, too. Linda stayed outside.

In the living room they found a man asleep on the couch. This was Voytek Frykowski. The man stretched sleepily, and asked: "What time is it?" Then he saw the gun Tex was holding in his face.

"Who are you? What are you doing here?" said Frykowski, alarmed now.

"I am the devil," was Tex's reply, "and I've come to do the devil's business." Then he ordered Sadie to tie the man up.

The girls found the other three occupants of the house and brought them at knife-point into the living room. All were too shocked to offer any resistance. Tex ordered them to lie face down on the floor. Jay Sebring complained, pointing out Sharon Tate's condition.

"Can't you see she's pregnant. Let her sit down."

Tex shot him.

Then they took the rope Tex had brought, and strung Sharon and Abigail Folger up to an overhead beam by their necks. "What are you going to do with us?" the women demanded.

"You are all going to die," said Tex.

Frykowski managed to get free from his bonds, and a mad struggle ensued. Sadie stabbed repeatedly at the man as they fought. Then Frykowski ran for the front door. Tex shot him once, then beat him over the head repeatedly with the butt of the gun. Standing outside, Linda saw Tex pursue Frykowski out of the front door, and stab him many times on the lawn.

Almost simultaneously Abigail Folger, who had also managed to get free, ran out of the french windows in Sharon's bedroom. She was bleeding profusely. Katie was after her with knife upraised. She caught up with Abigail on the lawn, and stabbed her until she lay still.

In Sadie Mae Glutz's chilling words: "Sharon was the last to die." The young actress pleaded for her life: "Please don't kill me. I want to have my baby." But the killers were without mercy. In the version she told the jury, Sadie claimed that she held Sharon while Tex stabbed her. But to her prison mates she said that she herself had stabbed the pregnant woman, and then tasted the blood.

"Wow, what a trip!" she told Virginia Graham in the Sybil Brand Institute. "To taste death and yet give life . . . It's warm and sticky and nice."

Outside Sadie found Tex checking that Abigail and Frykowski were dead. He told Sadie to go back inside and write "something that will shock the world".

Back in the living-room Sadie found the pregnant Sharon still bleeding. "I knew there was a living being inside of that body, and I wanted to but I didn't have the courage to go ahead and take it," she testified later. Instead Sadie took a towel, dipped it in Sharon Tate's blood, and wrote PIG on the door. Then they left.

Linda drove while the others changed out of their blood-soaked clothing. Tex was angry because Sadie had lost her knife. (It was this that the police found down the back of a chair.) The girls complained that their heads hurt from having their hair pulled in the struggle. Katie said her hand was bruised because she kept hitting bone when she stabbed.

Susan Atkins (left) stabbed Sharon Tate and said that she had wanted to rip the unborn baby from her womb. Linda Kasabian (right centre) spent 17 days on the stand, giving enough evidence to convict Manson and three of the other girls to the gas chamber. Leslie van Houten (right) held down Rosemary LaBianca, pulling up her nightdress while Katie stabbed the unfortunate woman in the back and buttocks 41 times.

Commenting on the prospect of the death penalty he said: "I'm already dead, have been all my life. I've spent 23 years in tombs that you built."

"I'm already dead"

Surprisingly, though, he turned down the chance to testify in front of the jury, saying: "I have already relieved all the pressure I had." Passing the girls, when he had finished his statement, Manson told them: "You don't have to testify now."

Right: San Quentin prison, California, has seen many a convicted murderer die in the gas chamber. The prospect of execution did not appear to worry Manson. "I have X'd myself from your world," he told the press.

The bloody clothes were thrown down a hill from Benedict Canyon Road (where police had failed, a TV crew found the bundle four months later). The weapons were similarly disposed of. They stopped on a side street to use a garden hose to wash off any remaining blood. A man came out and tried to stop them, but they got away from him. Later Rudolf Weber would come forward to say it was he who had seen the killers that night. Amazingly he even remembered the licence plate of the '59 Ford Mercury – GYY 435. Then they drove back to Spahn Ranch to find Manson waiting where they'd left him.

"What are you doing home so early?" he asked. They told him what they'd done.

"Boy," said Tex, "it sure was helter skelter."

The next evening the Family watched the TV news about the murders they'd committed. Afterwards Manson told them they were going out again, only this time he was coming with them.

"Last night was too messy," he told them. "This time I'm going to show you how to do it."

"I have tied them up"

Once again they took the '59 Ford. This time 17-year-old Clem (Steve Grogan) and 20-year-old Lulu (Leslie van Houten) came too. They drove around looking for a suitable house at random. They stopped in Pasadena, and Manson got out to take a look. A few minutes later he was back.

"He said he saw pictures of children through the window," Sadie said later, "and he didn't want to do that house."

Finally they pulled up outside a house where members of the Family, including Manson, had been to an acid party a year before. Manson told them to wait. He took a gun and went towards the house next door.

"I have the people tied up," he told the waiting group when he returned some time later. "They are very calm." Manson had used the leather thong he habitually wore around his neck to tie Leno LaBianca's hands.

Clearly Manson had told the LaBiancas they would not be harmed if they co-operated. It had been a cruel lie. Now he told Tex, Katie and Lulu to go into the house, and "paint a picture more gruesome than anybody has ever seen". Then he drove away with the others, telling Tex, Katie and Lulu to hitch back to Spahn when they'd finished their horrific night's work.

Inside Katie and Lulu took Rosemary LaBianca into the bedroom. When they heard Tex stabbing Leno in the other room, Rosemary started to scream: "What are you doing to my husband?" Lulu then held her down, while Katie stabbed her. The dying woman's last words were still: "What are you doing to my husband?"

Returning to the living-room, Katie took a carving fork from a drawer, stabbed Leno LaBianca with it several times, then stuck it into his stomach and watched, fascinated, as it waved back and forth. Then she carved the word WAR into his flesh.

When they'd written in blood on the walls and the fridge, they all took a shower, calmly ate water-melon and drank chocolate milk in the kitchen, then left.

Such was the story that state prosecutor Vincent Bugliosi had to tell the jury, when the trial of Charles Manson and his followers opened in LA's Hall of Justice on 24 July 1970. Denied access to the court, other female members of the Family kept a vigil for their Messiah on the pavement outside, while Manson did his best to disrupt proceedings inside.

The court refused him permission to conduct his own defence, so he appointed Irving Kanarek, notoriously the most obstructive and long-winded attorney in California. At times Manson refused to face the judge and was removed from court. The night before he faced the jury for the first time, he carved a bloody swastika into his forehead, declaring: "I have X'd myself from your world."

Slavish followers

Whatever he did, the three girls on trial, Sadie, Katie and Lulu, imitated his every action, thereby proving the prosecution's contention that they were wholly under the influence of the man they believed was Christ, and that though he hadn't struck a

Manson released to kill

Pimp and car thief Charles Manson is a prison survivor who has spent the majority of his life behind bars. He committed his first armed robbery at 13. Held in a juvenile centre, he sodomised one of the other boys, holding a razor to the throat of his terrified victim.

Manson could change his appearance but not his personality. Released on parole in 1958, he raped again – this time a woman – and was arrested for pimping.

Charles Milles Manson was a slight figure, standing just 5' 2" tall. He was born on 12 November 1934 in Cincinnati, Ohio, the illegitimate son of 16-year-old Kathleen Maddox and an unknown father. Kathleen brought a bastardy suit against a Colonel Scott in Ashland, Kentucky, which was settled out of court, implying that he could have been the father. But one set of Manson's prison records suggested otherwise. "Father," it reads, "... is alleged to have been a coloured cook by the name of Scott, with whom the boy's mother had been promiscuous at the time of pregnancy." Some have suggested that the fear that his father may have been black produced Manson's extreme hatred of black people.

Armed robbery

Brought up by his grandmother and a very strict and religious aunt, while his mother served time for armed robbery, Manson was soon in trouble. He was in and out of a variety of institutions, and committed his first blow himself, it was Charles Manson who was chiefly responsible for the Tate and LaBianca murders.

Initially it was to have been Sadie who would testify to how they tried to ignite the war between black and white – Helter Skelter. She had agreed to turn State's evidence in exchange for exemption from the death penalty. But even from prison, using the other girls as go-betweens, Manson was able to reach out and draw her back into the fold. So finally it was Linda Kasabian, who had only driven the car, who became the prosecution's star witness in exchange for full immunity.

Without such a deal there is no way the DA's office could have got a conviction at all. They had several pieces of evidence including an alleged remark of Manson's to a member of the Straight Satans that: "We knocked off five of them just the other night." They had Tex and Katie's fingerprints inside the Tate mansion. By now they also had a gun, and a witness who remembered a number plate. As far as corroborative evidence was concerned, that was about it. But with Linda's testimony they had enough to get convictions and death sentences for all four defendants, though the sentences were later commuted to life after the gas chamber was banned in California.

"Watch your own kids"

Facing the court with newly shaved heads, the girls spat defiance. "Better lock your doors and watch your own kids,"

Sadie told the jury who had just voted for her death. Manson himself who, according to one of his disciples, was "a changeling (who) seemed to change every time I saw him," had yet another face for the occasion. His hands trembled and he seemed close to tears.

"I accept this court as my father," he said meekly. "I have always done my best in my life to uphold the laws of my father, and I accept my father's judgement."

armed robbery at the age of 13. Later, in reform school, he raped a number of other boys.

In 1955 he graduated to federal crimes, when he was convicted of taking stolen cars across a state line, and served three years in Terminal Island. He was released on parole but was soon involved in pimping. In 1960 he had his parole revoked, and was sent to the US Penitentiary at McNeil Island for 10 years. By then he had married and divorced twice and fathered two children.

Church of Scientology

While in McNeil, Manson became a fanatical guitar player and fan of the Beatles, who first hit America in 1964. He also came under the influence of Alvin 'Creepy' Karpis, the sole survivor of the notorious Ma Baker gang who had killed 14 people. Karpis taught Manson to play steel guitar. Manson also became involved in Scientology, a religious cult started by science fiction writer L. Ron Hubbard. It seems to be the combination of these influences, as well as a few of his own ideas and some dabbling in satanism, that produced the weird and murderous philosophy that Charlie Manson peddled to his "Family".

Manson was released on 21 March 1967. That morning he begged the prison authorities to let him stay inside, saying prison was his home, and he didn't think he could make it in the outside world. He was 32 and had spent 17 years of his life in institutions. The authorities wouldn't listen.

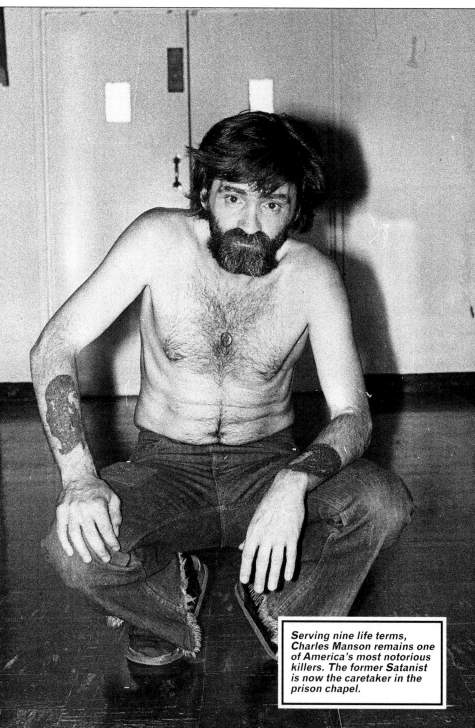

Serving nine life terms, Charles Manson remains one of America's most notorious killers. The former Satanist is now the caretaker in the prison chapel.

Although locally known as 'Nurse', Dorothea Nancy Waddingham had no nursing qualifications and the nursing home she ran was unlicensed.

NURSE NANCY'S DEADLY MEDICINE

Nurse Waddingham looked after two invalids who had left her all their money. But she could not wait for them to die.

Below: 32 Devon Drive was a large semi-detached house that Nurse Waddingham and her lover Ronald Sullivan advertised as a nursing home.

Ada Baguley's death on 11 September 1935 was not unexpected. Although only 50, she had been in poor health for months and was virtually bedridden. Her physician, Dr H. Manfield, gave cerebral haemorrhage as the cause of death; and Nurse Dorothea Nancy Waddingham and Ronald Sullivan, who ran the nursing home for the elderly at 32 Devon

Poisoned for her money

Ada Baguley was not fit enough to look after herself, let alone her 87-year-old mother. The two women moved into Nurse Waddingham's house in January 1935, agreeing to pay the sum of £3 per week. Nurse Waddingham soon decided that this was not enough, but the Baguley's money was all invested, providing them with a steady but fixed income.

Will changed

Ada was pressured into changing her will, leaving everything to Nurse Waddingham and Ronald Sullivan. But with four children to support and a fifth on the way, Nurse Waddingham was sorely tempted to hurry along the course of nature. First to die was elderly Louise Baguley, who was given an overdose of morphia within a week of her daughter signing the new will. Three months later, Ada received the same treatment.

Left: Ada Baguley in happier times. By the age of 50 she had ballooned to 17 stone and could not get into or out of bed unaided. She moved into Nurse Waddingham's home with her 87-year-old invalid mother.

Drive, Nottingham, where Ada was a patient, arranged for her to be cremated.

That might have been the end of the matter but for a curious letter written two weeks before Ada's death: "I desire to be cremated at my death for health reasons, and it is my wish to remain with Nurse until I die. It is my last wish that my relatives shall not know of my death." Although the letter wasn't in Ada's handwriting, she had signed it; and the last sentence had been squashed into too small a space as though an afterthought. Ada's signature had been witnessed by Sullivan.

Cremation halted

Dr Cyril Banks, Nottingham's Medical Officer of Health, was suspicious. Why would anyone *not* want their relatives to know of their death? Dr Banks refused to issue a cremation certificate until Ada's relatives had been traced and consulted. Adding to his disquiet were the facts that the nursing home was unlicensed and Dorothea Nancy Waddingham had never qualified as a State Registered Nurse, even though she was known to everyone as Nurse Waddingham.

It had been in January 1935 that Ada Baguley and her 87-year-old mother became patients at the home. They paid £3 a week for their joint keep and nursing care.

But within weeks Waddingham complained that £3 was too little for what the home was providing. The Baguleys' capital, however, was invested to provide their small income. They couldn't pay more.

The unhappy situation dragged on until May, when Ada tore up her will and instructed her solicitor to make a new one, leaving all her assets to Nurse Waddingham and Sullivan jointly, "in consideration that they have undertaken to look after me and my mother for and during our joint lives." Ada had £120 in her Midland Bank account; £500 in government stock; and £1,000 left to her by her father, the interest on which was to be paid to her mother for as long as she lived.

To the cash-strapped Waddingham it probably represented a small fortune. And a temptation. Perhaps she thought to herself: I might have to wait years for my inheritance, so why not hurry things along?

And that she did. Six days after the new will had been drawn up, Mrs Baguley died from 'cardiac degeneration', a condition often seen in elderly people. The doctor had no reason to suspect that she had been given a lethal dose of morphia.

Mrs Baguley was buried in Caunton churchyard. The weeks went by uneventfully. Then on 27 August Waddingham told Dr Manfield that Ada was having stomach pains. He wrote out a prescription for a kaolin mixture.

In September Waddingham began giving Ada morphia tablets with her medicine (tablets, she later claimed, the doctor had given her to give to Ada) – two tablets on 7 September, a Saturday; two on Sunday; two on Monday; two at lunchtime on Tuesday the 10th and two more that night.

The next day, 11 September, Sullivan telephoned Dr Manfield's surgery just before 9 a.m. The doctor was out on a call, so Sullivan left a message that Ada had been in a coma since 2 a.m. When the doctor arrived at the home at midday, Ada was dead.

After Dr Banks had read the curious letter, he called the police. They traced Ada's cousin, Laurence Baguley, who said he thought it unlikely that Ada would have wanted to be cremated as she had always opposed the idea.

Traces of morphia

Because cremation would destroy any poison that might have been administered, a post-mortem was carried out by Dr W. W. Taylor, senior assistant to the Nottingham Analyst. His examination revealed no sign of the cerebral haemorrhage said to have caused Ada's death. What it did reveal was a total of 3.192 grains of morphia – 2.59 grains in the stomach, 0.37 in the spleen and kidneys, 0.14 in the liver and 0.092 in the heart. (A fatal dose of the drug can be anything from 1 to 3 grains.)

As morphia begins to be expelled by the body in perspiration, urine and excreta soon after it is given, it was the opinion of the Home Office expert, Dr Roche Lynch, that considerably more morphia had been given than the three grains found. Clearly, Ada had died of morphia poisoning.

There was a growing suspicion that Ada's mother might also have been

Angel of Death

Waddingham and Ronald Sullivan seen at their so-called nursing home. The last time money had been tight, she had stolen a watch from her nursing maid and had also not paid the girl's wages. Nurse Waddingham had previously been bound over for passing bad cheques.

Dorothea Nancy Waddingham had nursed her husband through a long battle with cancer and, at the same time, she was looking after several patients at their newly-established 'nursing home'. Doctors had few reservations about her. Although unqualified, she seemed to be a very dedicated nurse.

However, the care of Ada Baguley and her mother required too much time and money. Doctors had prescribed morphia for an elderly resident who had died in February 1935, and Nurse Waddingham kept the tablets. Now she had the means, as well as the motive, to do away with Mrs Baguley and Ada.

opened on 24 February 1936 at Nottingham Assizes before Mr Justice Goddard. Both pleaded not guilty.

Mr Norman Birkett said the prosecution would show that the two had conspired to poison Mrs Baguley and Ada in order to benefit from the latter's will.

In order to convict Sullivan, however, the prosecution had to prove he had been a party to the murders; and Birkett had to admit that the prosecution did not know "the exact and precise parts played by each prisoner in the running of the nursing home".

Sullivan not guilty

The judge then asked Birkett what evidence the prosecution had against Sullivan. Birkett said they had no direct evidence against him "of either the possession of or the administering of morphine", but that there was "evidence against the female prisoner of both possession and administration . . . and evidence that the administration by the female prisoner was part of a common design and a common purpose."

The judge replied: "The only evidence against Sullivan is that he was in the house assisting in the taking about of the patients, raising them in and out of bed, wheeling them about and doing household work . . . The sum total of evidence against Sullivan comes to no more than that Sullivan *may* have been a participant, not that he *must* have been."

The judge then told Sullivan's counsel that in his judgment, "There is not sufficient evidence to justify me leaving the case against Sullivan to the jury." A verdict of not guilty was entered and Sullivan left the dock.

Doctor's testimony

The most damning evidence against Waddingham was Dr Manfield's testimony. There had never, he said, been an occasion for the use of morphia tablets in Ada's case.

Birkett asked him: "At the date you changed the medicine in August did you leave any tablets for Ada?" – "No." "Or at any other date did you leave tablets?" – "No. I never prescribed them; I never gave them."

From the witness box, Waddingham denied the prosecution's claim that she had not returned all the morphia tablets left with her when Mrs Kemp died. Her story of how she came by the morphia she had given Ada was that on 27 August she had told Dr Manfield that Ada was in pain; he had then prescribed another medicine and also gave her six tablets to give to Ada if her pain got worse – two each night with her medicine.

On 2 September, she went on, the doctor had asked if she had used the tablets; when she said no, he had then given her

poisoned. Her body was exhumed on 30 September. An autopsy by Dr Lynch revealed no evidence in the blood vessels that death had been caused by cardio-vascular degeneration. Instead, he found a quantity of pseudo-morphine (morphine that remains in the body for some months undergoes a chemical change and becomes pseudo-morphine).

Dr Lynch had no doubts that morphine "in excess of a medicinal dose" had been given; and that Mrs Baguley, like Ada, had died of it.

Nurse Waddingham and Sullivan were the obvious suspects. But how had they obtained large amounts of morphia? Enquiries by Detective Inspector Albert Pentland revealed that, in January, at the time the Baguleys had gone into the home, another patient, Mrs Kemp, was regularly given morphia tablets as a painkiller by her doctor. When Mrs Kemp had died, in February, a number of tablets could have been left over. Had these been used to kill the Baguleys?

The trial of Waddingham and Sullivan

Exhumed body yields vital clue

Not content with just poisoning her patient, Nurse Waddingham faked a letter from Ada Baguley. The letter said she wanted to be cremated and it was her last wish that her relatives would not be informed of her death. It aroused the suspicions of Nottingham's Officer of Health, Dr Cyril Banks, who arranged for the post-mortem that revealed Ada had been poisoned. The whole plot began to unravel. If Ada had died before her time, then what about her mother Louise?

Right: When 87-year-old Mrs Baguley died it was not unexpected. And until the death of her daughter, no-one suspected that the old lady's death was anything other than natural.

After it was discovered that Ada Baguley had been poisoned, the body of her mother was exhumed. The pathologist found strong evidence that she had also been given an overdose of morphia.

Left: The evidence against Ronald Sullivan was very weak and the case against him was dismissed. But Nurse Waddingham was clearly guilty, and it took the jury little more than two hours to decide on such a verdict. The jury recommended mercy, but the judge disagreed.

four more from a bottle in his pocket. He did not say what they were: "I took them to be half-grain morphine tablets, because some were given to me when I had pneumonia."

She had "administered morphia to Ada in accordance with the doctor who left 10 tablets with me for that purpose."

Someone was lying

Birkett, cross-examining, asked her why she had not told Detective Inspector Pentland she had given Ada morphia tablets when he had questioned her at the home. "I didn't say so because Dr Manfield told me not to."

Birkett: "Why should Dr Manfield tell you not to?"

Waddingham's reply was inaudible. Birkett went on: "Dr Manfield says he didn't give you any tablets. Do I understand you to say it is not true?" – "It is not true."

As Waddingham was virtually calling the doctor a liar, the judge recalled Dr Manfield. He reiterated firmly that he had not given morphine in any form to Ada Baguley. Clearly, someone was lying – and it was most unlikely that it was the doctor.

In his summing-up the judge said there were "important facts" in Waddingham's favour: she had not sought out the Baguleys, who had been on a month's trial and could have left at the end of that time; nor had Ada Baguley complained that she was not well looked after. But, equally, there were "grave and serious matters which might be said to tell against the prisoner". In particular the judge remarked on Waddingham's evidence that on the day before she died Ada had a breakfast of mush-

41

rooms; a lunch of two helpings of roast pork with apple sauce, baked potatoes and kidney beans, and Bakewell tart and tea afterwards.

"Can you, as men of common sense," the judge asked the jury, "think that anybody in their senses would give a woman suffering from such sharp abdominal pains that morphia had to be given for three nights, two helpings of pork, baked potatoes and fruit pie?"

Plea for mercy

After two hours 12 minutes the jury returned a verdict of guilty, with a strong recommendation for mercy. Nurse Waddingham, a short thickset figure in a black coat and maroon hat, stared ahead. "I am innocent," she said hoarsely.

As she was taken down she passed Sullivan on his way back to court to face the second charge, of murdering Mrs Baguley. He again pleaded not guilty. The prosecution could offer no evidence against him – and on the judge's direction he was acquitted.

The mercy recommendation went unheeded and Nurse Waddingham was hanged at Winson Green Prison, Birmingham, on 16 April 1936. □

Below: Opponents of capital punishment protested outside the prison where Nurse Waddingham was hanged.

Hanged for murder

Dorothea Nancy Waddingham, 36, was a Nottinghamshire farmer's daughter. She worked on the family farm and in a factory before becoming a ward-maid at the Workhouse Infirmary at Burton-on-Trent, Derbyshire, in her early 20s; there, she learned rudimentary nursing skills. In 1925 she was bound over for 12 months on a charge of obtaining two dresses from a shop by false pretences. That same year she married Thomas Willoughy Leech, a barman-waiter 25 years her senior.

In 1930 ill-health forced Leech to give up full-time work. Waddingham, now with two children, again resorted to crime – being bound over for two years for obtaining goods with a dud cheque.

Robbed the nursemaid

The couple then moved to West Bridgford, a suburb of Nottingham. Waddingham engaged a nursemaid for her children (there were now three) but never paid the girl's wages; she also pawned the girl's wristwatch for 10s 6d, keeping the money herself. She got three months' imprisonment for theft.

When she was released she set up a nursing home at the family home, calling herself Nurse Waddingham. A few months before Leech died of cancer he invited an old friend, Ronald Sullivan, to move in with them. Eventually Sullivan and Waddingham became lovers. That Waddingham had many good qualities is testified to by Sullivan, who said that during the final months of Leech's illness Waddingham "worked night and day attending to her patients, her children and her home . . . her last concern seemed to be for herself."

After Leech's death, Waddingham and Sullivan and the three children moved to 32 Devon Drive. The following year another child was born. A fifth child was born just five months before Waddingham's execution.

Last letter to lover

Days before she was hanged, Waddingham wrote to Sullivan, telling him: "Don't be afraid. I shall be alright, don't worry. I shall do my best for all." She also made a will: "Let Mary (aged three) have my machine, a piano, and the china cabinet. The other piano is to go to Maureen (five months). Edwin (nine), Alan (seven), Ronald (18 months) are to have a gold watch and chain, and half a sovereign each. Mary and Maureen are to have one gold wedding ring each, a gold watch each, gold brooches and dress rings each, and bracelets. Maureen a gold chain and Mary my pearls."

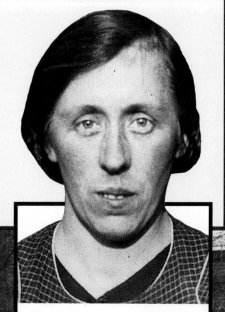

The jury recommended mercy because Nurse Waddingham was a mother of five and her youngest child was only a few months old. But she had shown no mercy to the invalids in her care, murdering them for their money.

RUTH SNYDER AND JUDD GRAY

GRANITE WOMAN AND PUTTY MAN

Ruth Snyder's husband was an obstacle to her love affair. To gain her freedom, she had to kill him.

Henry 'Judd' Gray and Ruth Mary Snyder first met in June 1925 at Henry's Scandinavian restaurant in Manhattan. It was a blind date which had been orchestrated by two of Ruth's friends, Karin Kaufman and Harry Folsom. Ruth and Judd made an odd couple, but they hit it off from the start. It was an attraction of opposites. Ruth was a tall, buxom, 31-year-old peroxide-blonde with a formidable appetite for drink and men. Judd was a 29-year-old underwear salesman for the Bien Jolie Corset Company, a short, skinny, timid man with pop-bottle spectacles.

Judd and Ruth spent their first hours together swapping personal histories. Ruth introduced herself by saying that she lived in Queen's Village, Long Island, with her husband, Albert, and their seven-year-old daughter, Lorraine. Albert, Ruth complained, was *much* older than she. He was a cold and insensitive man who spent all his time messing about in boats. In reality, Albert Snyder was only 41 and worked as the art editor for *Motor Boating* magazine, a job that required him to spend a fair

Thirty-three-year-old Ruth Snyder (left) and her lover Judd Gray (pictured below) committed a crime of passion in 1927 which has become one of the most famous in the history of American crime. Ruth and Judd had been conducting a passionate affair for over 18 months when Ruth, the dominant partner, decided that her husband had to die.

Ruth Snyder lived with her husband Albert in this comfortable middle-class home in Queens, a suburb of New York City.

cars, Jaguars or big American jobs. They had wardrobes full of elegant suits.

They saw themselves as showbusiness celebrities and liked to be seen out in West End clubs with stars like Barbara Windsor and Diana Dors, or boxing heroes like Henry Cooper and Freddie Mills. They were photographed posing with American singing star Judy Garland and famous aristocrats like Lord Boothby. They opened their own cabaret club, named after their initials, the Double R. They upheld all the East End ideals of the time. They dressed in Savile Row style, had influential friends and, best of all, they commanded respect, though in truth it was fear.

To try to balance their gangster image they made a big show of giving money to local boys' clubs or old folks' charities, and they doted on their mum, Violet. But under the sharp suits, the champagne and the showbiz pals, nothing could hide the fact that they were still dangerous, violent villains who settled most disputes with their fists, a bottle or a knife.

The Krays' 'court'

Some businessmen chose to defy the brothers' demands for money. The punishment was swift and vicious. Heavies were sent out to grab the unfortunate victims and bring them to the Krays' 'court', usually held in the back room of one of their favourite pubs. There, those who had dared to stand up to the twins were 'tried', and found guilty. Then their buttocks ▶

The Krays started life in a terraced house on Vallance Road in Bethnal Green (top). Moving up in the world, at their height they were running clubs in select locations like Wilton Row in Knightsbridge (below).

Family and Friends

Celebration at Vallance Road

The Kray family and friends at the front door of the family home in Vallance Road. Ronnie and Reggie have just been acquitted of demanding money with menaces. Central to the celebrations are mother Violet Kray and grandfather John Lee.

Lee had been a fairground and bare-knuckle fighter between the wars. Known as 'The Southpaw Cannonball', he was an East End character, noted for fairground tricks such as licking red-hot pokers. The twins got their love of fighting from him.

As the twins had grown from teenage thugs into violent criminals, Violet was always the first to defend them. She was quoted in later life as saying, "It's never them what starts the trouble, but because they're twins they stand out and they always get the blame." In return, the boys lavished love and attention on the woman they affectionately dubbed 'our Queen'.

At the height of their power in the 1960s, the worst crime in the Krays' eyes was failure to show respect to their mother. Stories were legion about the beatings and stabbings handed out to people deemed to have insulted Violet.

In Loving Memory
of my dear wife
Frances
who passed away
7th June, 1967 aged 23 years

If I could write the beauty
of your eyes,
And in fresh numbers
Number all your graces,
The Age to come would say:
This poet lies;
Such heavenly touches
ne'er touched earthly faces.

Mixing in society

Ronnie Kray is shown drinking in a club with Lord Boothby (far left) and Leslie Holt (right), a member of the Kray Firm. Reggie and Ronnie had money and a certain amount of style, which counted for a lot in London in the 1960s. Having money, they were potential investors in a number of business schemes, which brought them into contact with people in the city and in the government.

One business deal almost turned into a scandal. Rumours abounded in 1964 that Ronnie Kray was having a homosexual affair with Lord Boothby. However, the peer took the case to court, stating that he had only met Ronnie in connection with a business proposition. He won substantial damages from the *Daily Mirror* and *Sunday Mirror*.

Holt may have been the foundation of the rumours. At one stage, he tried to blackmail Boothby over the alleged affair. However, the court case cleared the peer's name. Curiously, Holt was soon to die in hospital, where he had been admitted for a wart operation.

Starting from the mean streets of London's East End, by the Swinging Sixties Reggie and Ronnie Kray had moved up to mix in high society with show-business stars. They never forgot where they came from, however, and their mother Violet remained the most important person in their lives.

Showbiz friends

Reggie is seen with Barbara Windsor after a first night party at one of the Krays' clubs. As club owners, the twins got to meet a large number of famous personalities from the world of sports and entertainment; people like Judy Garland and Henry Cooper were entertained by the Krays. To them, the brothers were rich businessmen, often doing charitable work. None of their famous acquaintances knew anything about the Krays' darker side. Reggie and Ronnie revelled in the extravagant social scene.

Reggie's wedding

Best man Ronnie kisses the bride, as Reggie marries 21-year-old Frances Shea in a lavish East End wedding in the spring of 1965.

The marriage was in trouble within a couple of months. Reggie had decidedly old-fashioned ideas about a woman's place, and Frances was expected to stay at home. She was not allowed to have a job.

Frances began to suffer from acute clinical depression, and in 1967 committed suicide with a barbiturate overdose. Reggie was shattered, and his behaviour changed for the worse. From being the more thoughtful of the brothers, as ready to negotiate as to fight, Reggie now became as sadistic and violent as his brother Ronnie.

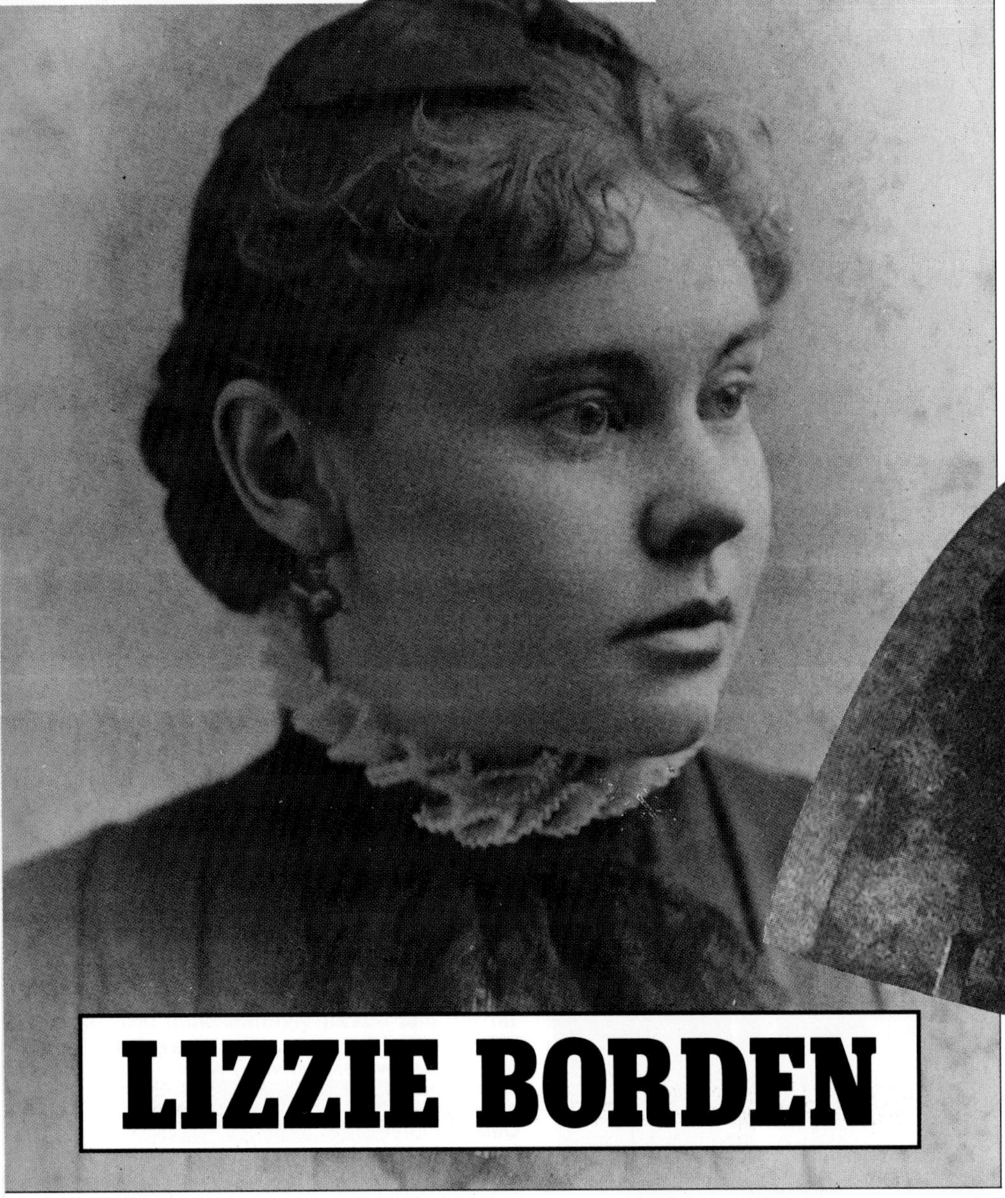

"Lizzie Borden took an axe
And gave her mother 40
   whacks.
When she saw what she
   had done
She gave her father 41."

The famous American rhyme commemorates a brutal crime. But was the prim New England spinster really a vicious killer?

Lizzie Borden was a blue-eyed Sunday school teacher. In August 1892 she was accused of taking the axe shown below and brutally hacking her father and stepmother to death.

LIZZIE BORDEN

TOOK AN AXE...

In the summer of 1892 Dr Seabury Bowen, of Fall River, Massachusetts, was summoned into the hot, stuffy, parlour of Andrew Jackson Borden by a near-hysterical housemaid, Bridget Sullivan. Borden, however, was beyond minding the heat. Someone had repeatedly smashed through the top of his head with an axe.

As Dr Bowen attended to Mr Borden, he heard the gasps of the housemaid and a neighbour who had ventured upstairs. Dr Bowen followed the noise to the guest room and was shocked to see the body of Andrew's wife, Abby Borden, face-down on the floor. The back of her skull was hacked open by multiple axe blows.

Officer George Allen of the Fall River police arrived on the scene soon after Dr Bowen. A glance at the two bodies sent

58

him back to the station in search of reinforcements. The police response was delayed as 4 August was the day of the annual department picnic. The police were followed by the press, who were shocked by what they saw. In the words of one of the first reporters on the scene: "I never saw a more horrible sight and I have walked over battlefields where thousands were dead and mangled."

Axed to death

The Falls River police were faced with the dual problem of two substantial citizens axed to death in their home and an increasing number of reporters writing about it for the next day's papers. They badly needed a suspect.

They did not have to look far. Andrew

Jackson Borden's daughter, Miss Lizzie Borden, tastefully attired in a demure, light-blue summer dress, was politely assisting the police with their enquiries. She was, indeed, the only person who admitted to being inside the house for much of the morning of the two murders. The Fall River police focused on Lizzie in the absence of what they saw as better suspects.

The police did not, however, take her in on the spot. Many of the early reports suggested a stranger, perhaps a thwarted robber. Indeed, Lizzie, along with her sister Emma, advertised for information on this mysterious felon and offered a reward if the information led to capture.

It was only after the coroner's inquest – and reports of a different blue dress being consigned to the furnace – that Lizzie was arrested. Without an attorney present, Lizzie's story seemed to falter. The stage was now set for one of the most significant American criminal trials of the Victorian era.

Charged with murder

Lizzie was brought to trial for the capital murder of her parents in the Massachusetts Superior Court in nearby New Bedford. It was June 1893 by the time the pretrial discovery had been completed. Both the prosecution and the defence had brought in heavyweight specialists.

The prosecution attempted to set the scene not just for disgusting behaviour, but for parricide. It depicted the sights and smells of the Borden home for those present in the courtroom. Andrew Jackson Borden had not been fond of soap and water and refused to spend money on the

Below: Andrew Borden was widowed soon after his daughter was born, and remarried when Lizzie was four. Abby, his greedy second wife, was hated by her stepchildren.

newfangled indoor plumbing that Lizzie wanted. Instead, he manfully emptied the slop buckets of human waste in the back yard, next to the pear tree, every morning. Then he collected the fallen pears for breakfast.

Family hostility

But the testimony showed that thicker than the stench in the house was the hostility. Doors throughout the Borden house were locked or barricaded with heavy furniture and reinforced with the barbed wire of long silences and thinly veiled contempt. Andrew and Abby pitted their wits against Lizzie and Emma. Not only did they not talk together, they would not eat together either. Bridget had to serve each meal twice, no doubt reconsidering the

Unhappy families

A century after the trial, there is still much room for speculation. Was there information that did not appear in the transcript that motivated the judge to take the extraordinary step of delivering a summing-up to the jury that many believe ensured Lizzie's acquittal? It could easily have been mere sentiment or ethnic and class prejudice in favour of the defendant: certainly none of these components was in short supply in New England in 1892. But on two fronts – the scientific evidence and the possible motivation for the crimes – it may have been the case that there was more substance to Judge Dewey's actions.

Family abuse

Today, the frequency of incest in dysfunctional families, and of sexual abuse in employer/employee relationships and their potentially devastating impact is well recognised. But in 1892, it was hard for the good citizens of Fall River, believers in progress and rationality, to even accept that such things existed except among the savage and depraved, let alone the respectable upper-middle class. It was all part of the innocence of that age. Did Judge Dewey, too, believe that the air of Fall River was much purer without having Andrew Jackson Borden around to breathe it? If so, that would also explain his summing up to the jury.

Today, some feminists see Lizzie as a survivor and a heroine, striking back against parental abuse and patriarchal oppression, if not outright sexual molestation. Was Andrew sexually abusing Lizzie, Bridget, or both? Again, there is no evidence, but the pattern of the case fits one that has become all too familiar in an age that is much more aware of the prevalence of such relationships.

Iron-fisted control

If Bridget was the victim, Andrew would hardly have been the first or the last proper upper-middle class Victorian who 'had his way' with the housemaid. For Lizzie, the situation in the Borden house certainly fits many elements of a disturbingly common profile of father-daughter incest. Andrew, for all his dirt and miserly ways, thought of himself as always right. He maintained iron-fisted control over the house and all in it, and blocked any 'outsiders' from affecting it. Lizzie had been 'daddy's special girl'. Their relationship had been a close one in the past: she had given him a gold ring that he wore to the end of his life. Such ambiguous relationships are now seen to be the common result of incest. Many survivors do not display immediate revulsion against the perpetrator but deny, displace, or blame themselves, with the issue only surfacing for resolution through a long and painful process.

Protecting the maid

Others have sought the key in Lizzie's relationship with Bridget. The late 19th century was tolerant of intimate friendships between women – it was that common in Massachusetts it was known as 'Boston marriage' – but not between proper White Anglo-Saxon Protestant middle class ladies and Irish maidservants. From her testimony at the trial, it is obvious that Bridget thought the world of Lizzie. If Lizzie had been willing to implicate Bridget in the murders, she would probably have cleared herself. There would have been little hesitation in hanging an Irish maidservant in those days. Even if she had been required to gratify Andrew whenever Abby was out of the house, and had finally snapped at the horror and degradation of it, this would not have gone over well as part of plea for clemency. The judges of the day could probably imagine their own maidservants wielding the axe.

Whatever her relation with Bridget, Lizzie was not one for public displays of affection. She did not mellow until she was middle aged, when she struck up a tumultuous and close friendship with an actress, Nance O'Neill.

wisdom of having exchanged the poverty of Ireland for the misery of the Borden house as she did so.

The prosecution's case tried to show that Lizzie saw Abby as pursuing her father's money with the same zeal that she

Below: When Lizzie came to trial, friends and relatives rallied round to support her. Those present included elder sister Emma (second from the left) and the Reverend Mr Buck (centre), who was minister at the church that the Borden family attended.

Andrew Borden was found in the sitting room. He had no self-defence wounds on his arms, indicating that he had most likely been the victim of a surprise attack.

The house of death

Left: Abby Borden's battered body was found in an upstairs guest room. She had probably been killed an hour before her husband.

VIEW OF THE VICINITY OF THE MURDERS.

I. Borden house.
II. Borden barn.
III. The well.
IV. Fence with barbed wire on top.
V. Side entrance.
VI. Churchill residence.
VII. Dr. Bowen's house.
VIII. Dr. Chagnon's house.
IX. Kelley house.
X. Yard from which officers watched the Borden house.
XI. Kelley's barn.
XII. Pear orchard.

The Borden house stood in its own small garden. At the rear was the barn (number II in the diagram to the left) where Lizzie claimed she had been working when the murders occurred.

pursued hot dinners. When Andrew put one of his rental properties in Abby's name, Lizzie, backed up by Emma, demanded that his daughters receive equal treatment. Lizzie was quickly gaining a reputation for demanding changes in the status quo. She had, the year before, reportedly committed a family robbery, stealing some of Abby's jewels and Andrew's cash.

The prosecution, however, was denied its strongest piece of evidence. A week before the murders, as it appeared likely that Andrew would be signing over the deeds to some more property to Abby, Lizzie developed an interest in chemistry and tried to purchase prussic acid, 'to kill moths'. The chemist refused. However, while the chemist's testimony had been given at the coroner's inquest, at the trial it was ruled inadmissible against Lizzie, as having no probative value. Further, none of Lizzie's inconsistent testimony at the inquest was allowed to be admitted into evidence, due to her lack of counsel. It was a serious blow for the prosecution's case.

Defence case

The defence kept Lizzie off the stand to avoid her earlier, inconsistent testimony at the inquest being brought before the jury. Nor was the defence willing to finger any other person – or persons – as the supposed murderer. They instead made much

of Lizzie's upstanding character and charitable work.

Both the prosecution and the defence agreed on the events immediately before the axes dropped. On Tuesday 4 August, the Bordens ate breakfast separately. Andrew then went into town and Bridget, who was not feeling well, was put to cleaning windows, despite the oppressive heat. Two weeks earlier Emma had scurried out of town to visit friends. Abby, before going out to sign the deeds relating to her latest property grab, went upstairs to the guest room. There, at what the prosecution later alleged was about 9.00 a.m., she died like a swine in a slaughterhouse.

When Andrew came home, he did not look for his wife as he thought she was out. Instead he lay down on the settee in the parlour. Whatever he was doing there, it was terminated, at what the prosecution claimed was about 10.30. a.m., by the same avenging axe.

Misleading evidence

Despite this strong case, the prosecution appeared almost apologetic throughout the trial for prosecuting Lizzie. This could have been partly due to an awareness of the weakness of its case. The evidence suggested an hour-and-a-half gap between the two killings, which shifted the focus to

Right: Lizzie Borden emerged from her trial at the New Bedford Court House (below) as a famous woman. People were delighted that she had gone free – none more than Lizzie herself, who could now inherit her father's immense wealth.

the one suspect the police had managed to find: Lizzie. Had the defence been wide awake, it could have shown that the forensic evidence was equally consistent with both victims being killed at the same time, possibly by a surprised burglar or one of Andrew's enemies.

Some of the prosecution's weakness may not have been simply a desire to avoid its bad forensics being put to the test. It may also have been a reluctance to send a church-going young lady to the gallows. It would serve as a bad example to the new immigrants flooding into the country to show White Anglo-Saxon Protestants hacking each other apart. With the lower classes increasingly contending for political

Lizzie's trial

The trial of Lizzie Borden opened in June 1893. She was defended by George D. Robinson, seen standing in the sketch above. Robinson was not an experienced lawyer, but as a three-times former governor of Massachusetts his opinions carried considerable weight.

power – 1892 was a year of violent strikes – the upper middle classes, of which the Bordens were members, may have been feeling insecure.

At the conclusion of both cases, Justice Justin Dewey, the trial judge, gave a summing-up to the jury that went far beyond that almost ever seen in an American criminal trial (British judges are allowed much more scope in their summing-up to the jury to comment on the evidence). The usual rule is that it is impermissible for a judge to direct a jury on the facts of the case or, more significantly, even indirectly comment on the evidence, but Justice Dewey did both, skilfully and forcefully. Many attribute Lizzie's acquittal to his actions.

Acquitted of murder

But Lizzie Borden's acquittal of the double axe murder of her parents, in one of the most celebrated trials of the age, settled nothing. To the end of Lizzie's days, most Americans, including her neighbours in Fall River where she defiantly remained for the rest of her life, were convinced by the prosecution's evidence that she had wielded the axe.

Did Lizzie do it?

Miss Lizzie Borden has entered the pages of American history. The 32-year-old Sunday school teacher is commemorated in the rhyme known to every American child:

> *Lizzie Borden took an axe*
> *And gave her mother 40 whacks*
> *When she saw what she had done*
> *She gave her father 41.*

More substantially, 17 books, movies, an opera and even a ballet have appeared about Lizzie. Her crime was obviously one so worth caring about that it still exerts interest today when most American cities have had many more recent double murders. No-one, however, has the answer to the question: Did she do it? And if she did not, who did?

Whoever wielded the axe – Lizzie, the young, Irish housemaid Bridget Sullivan, Andrew's illegitimate son William, a

In the late autumn of 1892, No. 92 Second Street was a tourist attraction. People were drawn to the site by the horrifying crime committed within, and public interest has not waned in the ensuing century.

Bridget Sullivan was very close to Lizzie Borden. So close, in fact, that many felt that it was the Irish maid who had actually committed the murders.

conspiracy of two or more of these, or some unknown criminal – they doubtless felt that Andrew Jackson Borden 'had it coming'. Historical judgements on Lizzie's father range from a grasping, miserly patriarch who tyrannised his two daughters, shunned his illegitimate son, and had made his money selling over-priced funerals to the grieving families of the poor, to more recent theories that he was a nasty piece of work, who abused either or both his daughter Lizzie and Bridget Sullivan.

Hypochondriac stepmother

Lizzie's stepmother Abby Borden was a porcine hypochondriac with squinting black eyes. She seemed to be Andrew's match when it came to a willingness to chase a dollar to hell, but ended up with her share of the axe rather than Andrew's $500,000 estate. Opinions on Abby also vary from a greedy fortune hunter who latched onto the hateful old man for his money, to a willing partner of his dark and unnatural lusts.

However, it was not the murders in Fall River that seized the public's imagination in 1892 but the accused murderess. To the Americans of that era the Bordens' murder exerted a compelling fascination – complete with hints of resentment, greed, forbidden love, unnatural lust, parricide and incest, all covered in a thick coat of middle class rectitude. The media played its part in sensationalising the crime and trial: circulation wars between newspapers for the pennies of an increasingly literate public were becoming more and more vicious. While murder was not rare, this one was obviously unique.

Blue-eyed axe-murderess

Lizzie – the newspapers' blue-eyed virgin axe-murderess – was physically unremarkable. She had a well-upholstered 1892 'good figure', complete with a fashionable double chin. Never close to her stepmother, who married Andrew Borden when Lizzie was four years old, she was raised by her sister Emma. It has been said she had been given a nickname instead of affection.

She was not well educated (she left school at 16), nor did she associate with men other than the rigidly upright water-drinking New England clergymen who shared her charitable good works. But she may well have held the secret to what happened in the foully stinking Borden house that morning.

In the end, it was a jury of solid New England farmers, men who had been brought up to believe that church-going middle-class women could do no wrong, who found Lizzie Borden innocent.

JOHN HAIGH
The Acid Bath
MURDERER

Haigh dissolved his victims' bodies in drums of concentrated sulphuric acid. He believed that if the police could find no bodies, he could not be convicted of murder.

Always smartly turned out, Haigh posed as a successful company director. But he was a con-man with convictions for fraud and theft.

John Haigh was known to the other residents of Kensington's Onslow Court Hotel as a successful businessman. He wore smart suits and drove a sports car, but his money did not come from his business. It came from murder.

When the residents of the Onslow Court Hotel came down for breakfast on the morning of 19 February 1949, they immediately noticed that one of their number was missing. Mrs Olive Durand-Deacon, a wealthy 69-year-old widow, had been a permanent resident at the hotel for some years and was noted for her punctiliousness. It was unlike her to be late for a meal.

Mrs Constance Lane, another resident and a close friend of Mrs Durand-Deacon, was particularly concerned and decided to make a few discreet enquiries. Her concern deepened when the hotel's chambermaid told her that Mrs Durand-Deacon's bed had not been slept in.

Later that morning Mrs Lane was approached by another of the Onslow Court's residents, Mr John George Haigh. Haigh was something of an odd man out at this genteel South Kensington establishment, a private hotel which was almost exclusively the preserve of elderly, well-heeled, upper-class ladies. It was not that his presence was resented by the other residents. On the contrary, most of the Onslow Court ladies found the dapper 39-year-old engineer handsome, charming and meticulously well mannered. Mrs Durand-Deacon was a particular fan of his and the two of them had taken to spending long hours huddled together in the lounge, 'talking business'.

Haigh asked Mrs Lane if she knew Mrs Durand-Deacon's whereabouts, saying that they had had an appointment the previous day and that Mrs Durand-Deacon had failed to show up. He did so hope she was all right.

Missed appointment

Mrs Lane already knew about the appointment. She had seen Mrs Durand-Deacon just as she was about to leave the hotel, and she'd said she was on her way to Haigh's factory in Crawley to discuss a business project. Mrs Lane could not understand how she could have "failed to show up".

Mrs Lane had never liked Haigh. He was too oily for her taste, and his involvement with Mrs Durand-Deacon had always made her uneasy. She instinctively mistrusted him, and now she had a creeping feeling that something was seriously amiss.

Mrs Lane toyed with the idea of going to

63

"I have a sense that he is 'wrong'..."

Haigh's smarmy manner may have impressed the old ladies at the Onslow Court Hotel but it cut no ice with Woman Police Sergeant Alexandra Lambourne. She sensed he was a villain and prompted the CID to investigate him. It turned out that Haigh had obtained money on hire-purchase agreements using false addresses; that he was a car thief and a con-man who had served three jail sentences.

Above: Haigh and Mrs Constance Lane went to Chelsea police station to report the disappearance of Mrs Durand-Deacon. He alone knew where she was – dissolving in acid in his Crawley workshop.

Above: The Onslow Court Hotel was a private hotel mostly occupied by elderly women. Haigh had befriended wealthy resident Mrs Durand-Deacon.

Left: Haigh at the wheel of the Alvis car in which he drove to report Mrs Durand-Deacon's 'mysterious' disappearance. The 69-year-old widow (inset) had been lured to her death for £110-worth of jewellery and a Persian lamb coat.

the police but realised that there might be some perfectly innocent reason for Mrs Durand-Deacon's absence. So, anxious not to embarrass her friend or make a fool of herself, she decided to wait.

The following morning, 20 February, there was still no sign of Mrs Durand-Deacon. Mrs Lane was at breakfast, pondering her next move, when she was again approached by Haigh, expressing concern. Mrs Lane was suddenly galvanised into action. She told Haigh that she was going down to the police station to fill out a missing persons report, and that she would like him to go with her. Haigh had little choice but to agree, and he offered to drive them both down to Chelsea police station.

Fingernail scheme

The report Haigh made to the police was plausible enough. According to him, Mrs Durand-Deacon had approached him for some technical advice. She was thinking of starting a business, designing and manufacturing artificial fingernails. She had already made some paper prototypes but

she knew absolutely nothing about the technical side of things. Being an engineer, perhaps he, Haigh, could give her a few pointers?

In reality, Haigh said, Mrs Durand-Deacon's idea was a commercial non-starter in ration-bound post-war England, but he had not wanted to hurt her feelings and had said he would be delighted to help. They had planned to drive down to his workshop in Crawley to look at some materials from which the nails could be made. He had arranged to meet Mrs Durand-Deacon on the afternoon of 18 February at 2.30 p.m. outside the Army and Navy Stores in Victoria Street. He had waited there until 3.30 p.m., but she had not arrived and he had driven down to Sussex alone. He was, of course, extremely concerned about Mrs Durand-Deacon's welfare, and would do anything he could to help the police to locate her. The police thanked Haigh for his co-operation and said that they would be in touch if they thought of anything else.

Haigh drove Mrs Lane back to the Onslow Court Hotel, hoping that he would

hear no more of the matter. Four days later, however, on Thursday 24 February, Woman Police Sergeant Alexandra Lambourne went to the hotel to gather additional background information on Mrs Durand-Deacon. She interviewed Haigh at some length and, like Mrs Lane, was immediately repelled by his superficial charm and unctuous concern for the well-being of the missing widow. She was an experienced police officer and was convinced that Haigh was lying.

WPS Lambourne had nothing to back up this gut feeling, but she felt strongly enough about it to mention it in her report to her Divisional Detective Inspector, Shelley Symes. "Apart from the fact I do not like the man Haigh and his mannerisms," she wrote, "I have a sense that he is 'wrong', and there may be a case behind the whole business."

Symes had enough respect for Sergeant Lambourne's judgement to ask the Criminal Record Division at Scotland Yard to run a check on Haigh. Within a matter of hours, they came back to him with a file which showed that John George Haigh had been jailed three times, twice for obtaining money by fraud and once for theft. Further enquiries in London and Sussex showed that he owed substantial sums of money, and that he was in arrears with his bill at the Onslow Court Hotel.

On Saturday 26 February, Sergeant Pat Heslin and Police Sergeant Appleton of the

Sussex Constabulary went to see Mr Edward Jones, owner of Hurstlea Products, a small engineering company located in Giles Yard off Leopold Road in Crawley. Jones told the police that he had known John Haigh for some years and over the past few months he had let him have the use of a storehouse at the back of the factory for a peppercorn rent. Haigh had been using the premises for some sort of 'experimental work', but had never said precisely what this entailed.

The police were anxious to look round the shed, but Jones told them that Haigh had the only set of keys. So Heslin prised the padlock off the door of the small brick-built shed. At first glance the whitewashed interior looked ordinary enough. There was the usual clutter – paint pots, old bits of wood, a couple of work benches, carboys of chemicals, protective clothing – but then something caught the sergeant's eye. On one of the workbenches there was a small hat box and an expensive leather briefcase. They simply didn't belong.

Loaded gun

Heslin looked through the case and found a variety of papers and documents, including ration books and clothing coupons. The contents of the hat box included several passports, driving licences and diaries, a cheque book and a marriage certificate, none of which bore the name of Haigh. At the bottom of the box was the most alarming find of all, a .38 Enfield revolver and a small white envelope containing eight bullets.

The following evening, 27 February, John Haigh was invited back to Chelsea police station to answer further questions. Haigh appeared to be totally unconcerned as he was installed in the Divisional Detective's office with a cup of tea. He had actually dozed off by the time Detective Inspector Symes, Inspector Albert Webb and Superintendent Barratt arrived to interview him at 7.30 p.m.

They came at him well armed with evidence. Not only did they have the obvious-ly stolen documents from the Crawley workshop, they had also traced Mrs Durand-Deacon's jewellery to a dealer in Horsham, Sussex. The dealer's description of the seller matched John Haigh precisely, as did that of a dry-cleaner to whom he had apparently taken Mrs Durand-Deacon's Persian lamb coat.

Confronted with this evidence, Haigh puffed on a cigarette, and said calmly: "I

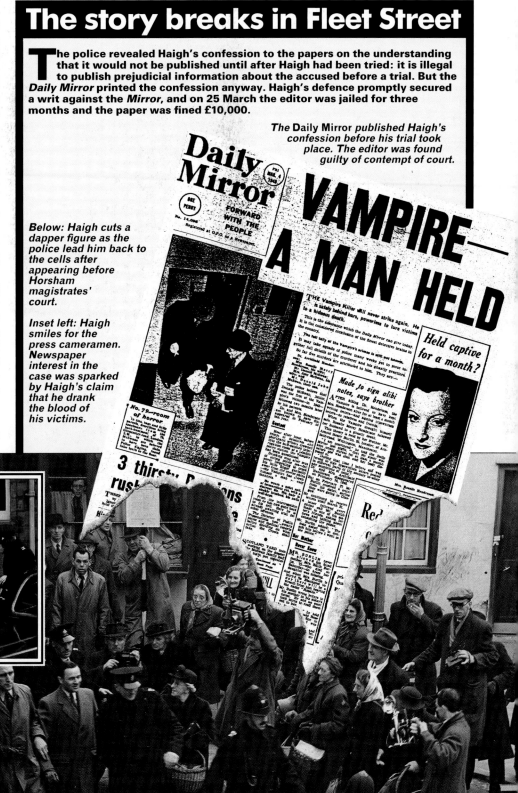

The story breaks in Fleet Street

The police revealed Haigh's confession to the papers on the understanding that it would not be published until after Haigh had been tried: it is illegal to publish prejudicial information about the accused before a trial. But the *Daily Mirror* printed the confession anyway. Haigh's defence promptly secured a writ against the *Mirror,* and on 25 March the editor was jailed for three months and the paper was fined £10,000.

The Daily Mirror published Haigh's confession before his trial took place. The editor was found guilty of contempt of court.

Below: Haigh cuts a dapper figure as the police lead him back to the cells after appearing before Horsham magistrates' court.

Inset left: Haigh smiles for the press cameramen. Newspaper interest in the case was sparked by Haigh's claim that he drank the blood of his victims.

can see you know what you're talking about. I admit the coat belonged to Mrs Durand-Deacon and that I sold her jewellery."

"How did you come by the property," asked Symes, "and where is Mrs Durand-Deacon?"

Haigh thought for a while before replying. "It's a long story," he confided. "It's one of blackmail and I shall have to implicate many others."

Just then, the telephone rang and Symes and Barratt were summoned from the room. Left alone with Inspector Webb, the most junior of his interrogators, Haigh switched tack. "Tell me frankly," he asked, "what are the chances of anyone being released from Broadmoor?"

Destroyed with acid

Webb's immediate reaction to Haigh's extraordinary question was to caution him and advise him of his rights. Haigh dismissed the warning with a wave of the hand. "If I told you the truth," he continued, "you would not believe it. It is too fantastic for belief. I will tell you all about it. Mrs Durand-Deacon no longer exists. She has disappeared completely and no trace of her can ever be found. I have destroyed her with acid. You will find the sludge that remains at Leopold Road. Every trace has gone.

"How can you prove a murder if there is no body?" Haigh added, obviously pleased with himself.

Webb's first reaction to Haigh's confession was to disbelieve it. It was simply too fantastic, too grotesque. Haigh was obviously setting himself up for an insanity plea. After all, he had already mentioned Broadmoor.

When Symes and Barratt returned to the interview room, Webb asked Haigh to repeat what he had said. Haigh did so. Symes cautioned him again, but there was no stopping Haigh now. He talked for two and a half hours, as Inspector Symes wrote.

He described the events of Friday 18 February in meticulous detail. He told how he had picked up Mrs Durand-Deacon in his Alvis and driven her down to Crawley. He described how she had bent over her handbag to extract her fingernail designs and how, as she turned away from him, he had pulled a .38 Enfield revolver from his jacket pocket and shot her through the nape of the neck, killing her instantly. Haigh went on to describe how he had then knelt by his victim's body, made an incision in her neck, gathered a few inches of her still coursing blood in a glass, and drunk it.

Having slaked his thirst, Haigh claimed he had gathered together Mrs Durand-Deacon's valuables – the Persian lamb coat, rings, a necklace, earrings and a gold crucifix – and stowed them in his car.

He had then proceeded to get rid of the body. The clutter which the police found in the workshop was in fact the paraphernalia of Mrs Durand-Deacon's material destruction – carboys of sulphuric acid, a specially lined metal drum, rubber gloves and apron, a gas mask and a stirrup pump. Haigh had needed all these things in order to dissolve the body. He had known precisely what to do. He had done it before.

Dressed to kill

He had laid the 45-gallon drum on its side and pushed Mrs Durand-Deacon's head and shoulders inside, and then righted the drum so that the whole body slumped down to the bottom. He had then gone to the 'Ye Olde Ancient Priors' restaurant in Crawley and ordered a poached egg on toast and a cup of tea. On his return he had donned his rubber apron, gloves, wellington boots and gas mask, and poured concentrated sulphuric acid into the drum. "The question of getting the right amount was only learned by experience," he boasted.

Haigh said he had adjusted the acid level to cover the entire body by using a stirrup pump. Once satisfied, all he had to do was

Right: Haigh found, by experience, that after 20 minutes the heat generated by the action of sulphuric acid on a body made the drum too hot to touch. The intense heat melts human bones completely within a few days.

Left: The storehouse at the back of Hurstlea Products was where Haigh dissolved the body.

Below: The dismal interior became known as 'The Acid Bath Factory' when the gruesome details of the story were revealed.

Victim of the acid bath

Mrs Durand-Deacon was standing at the workbench when Haigh stepped up behind her and shot her dead. He removed her rings, necklace, earrings and fur coat before rolling her body into the drum for disposal.

Haigh's Death Factory

Haigh shot dead 69-year-old Olive Durand-Deacon on Friday 18 February 1949. Then he rolled her body into an empty 45-gallon drum lying on the floor of the workshop. To fortify himself for the task ahead, Haigh then popped over the road to the 'Ye Olde Ancient Priors' for a cup of tea and a poached egg on toast. On his return he donned his sinister set of protective clothing. He pumped in enough acid to cover the body, and then, after he had dinner, he drove back to London. Haigh returned to the workshop over the weekend to monitor the process, and emptied the sludge into the yard on Monday. After another few days, little evidence would have remained.

Pathologist Dr Keith Simpson (above) studies the wasteland where he found enough bodily remains to identify Mrs Durand-Deacon. Four hundred and seventy-five pounds of topsoil and acid sludge were packed into boxes and taken away for examination (right).

wait for the flesh and bone to dissolve. He knew this would take at least two days, and so he then went for dinner at The George Hotel's restaurant, before driving back to the Onslow Court Hotel.

Haigh went on to describe how, on the following Monday, he had disposed of his victim's jewellery for £110, and then returned to Crawley and emptied the sludge – Mrs Durand-Deacon's decomposed body – out of the drum with a bucket, and poured it on to some waste ground at the back of the shed.

Five other murders

The police said nothing as Haigh told his terrible story of murder and theft, vampirism and genteel cups of tea. When he had finished with his version of the demise of Mrs Durand-Deacon, Haigh moved back in time and, by the early hours of 1 March, he had also confessed to five other murders.

The first, he claimed, had been committed on 9 September 1944. The victim had been an old acquaintance, William McSwan. He had killed him in a basement flat in Gloucester Road. A year later, he had lured William's parents, Donald and Amy McSwan, to the same flat, and had beaten them to death. He had forged Donald's signature to gain power of attorney over their estate.

While selling one of their properties some time in February 1948, he had met Dr Archibald Henderson and his wife Rosalie. He had killed them in the storeroom in Giles Yard.

In each case, he had acquired money or other property belonging to his victims by skilful forgery and deception. Years after he had disposed of their remains, he had written forged personal and business letters, "successfully staving off enquiries from relatives, friends and associates".

Haigh added that he had destroyed all the bodies by means of his acid bath method after drinking a glass of their blood.

The arrest of John Haigh caused an im-

Left: The gun used to kill Mrs Durand-Deacon belonged to Dr Henderson, a former army doctor and one of Haigh's earlier victims.

mediate public sensation. Stories of acid baths, vampirism and murder are the stuff of which the tabloid newspapers are made. Haigh's remand at Horsham magistrates' court drew huge crowds, predominantly composed of jeering women.

On 4 March, after being transferred from the Chelsea police cells to Lewes Prison, Haigh sprang more surprises. He asked to see Inspector Webb, with whom

he clearly felt some sort of affinity. He confided in the young detective that he had committed three murders which he hadn't mentioned in his earlier statement – a woman and a youth in west London, and a girl in Eastbourne. This brought his total to nine.

The police, however, were having their time cut out establishing a case against Haigh for the murder of Mrs Durand-Deacon. Even though he had admitted to the crime, to be certain of a conviction the

"I drank their blood"

By the time Haigh was tried for the murder of Mrs Durand-Deacon, there was little doubt about his guilt. The only way he could have escaped the gallows was if the jury had found him insane. While Haigh himself never claimed to be insane, he almost certainly saw a verdict of insanity as a possible means of escape. "What are the chances of anyone being released from Broadmoor?" he had asked Detective Inspector Albert Webb, before he had even been charged with murder.

Was he insane?

Haigh's defence team introduced all sorts of bizarre evidence which seemed to support the idea that their client was in fact insane. There were stories of his vampirism, of his drinking his own urine while in prison, and of his terrible visions and nightmares. They introduced psychiatrist Dr Henry Yellowlees as an expert witness. Yellowlees stated that Haigh was suffering from paranoia, but could not say with any conviction that Haigh was unable to differentiate between right and wrong.

The general feeling both inside and outside court was that Haigh had made a conscious decision to drink blood and urine, and had invented his own nightmare in a calculated effort to save his own neck. If this was true, what could drive an obviously intelligent,

Haigh tried to avoid the death penalty by pleading insanity, but his 'vampire' stories failed to convince the jury.

apparently rational man to commit such horrific crimes? While it is true that he profited from his killing, the profit was so paltry that it cannot be seen as a satisfactory motive.

One contemporary psychiatrist came up with a suggestion. "It is possible," he said, "that Haigh set out to feign insanity, not knowing that he was already mad."

prosecution needed proof that she was in fact dead, and that Haigh had indeed killed her.

The Home Office pathologist Dr Keith Simpson first carried out routine blood tests at the workshop in Crawley and established that they were of the same group as Mrs Durand-Deacon. Then he turned his attention to the wasteland where Haigh claimed to have deposited the 'sludge' from his acid bath. Soon he found a stone 'the size of a cherry'. It was a gall-stone. Simpson handed it to Detective Sergeant Heslin, saying: "There you are, Sergeant, that's the first trace of a human body." Heslin congratulated the doctor on his good luck.

"It wasn't luck," Simpson snapped, "I was looking for it. Women of Mrs Durand-Deacon's age and habits – 69 and fairly plump – are prone to gallstones."

Simpson soon found more human remains, fragments of a left foot which he managed to reconstruct and cast in plaster. The cast fitted one of Mrs Durand-Deacon's shoes perfectly. Then he found fragments of pelvic bones and two discs from a lower spinal column.

Victim's belongings

He discovered other non-human remains – the handle of a handbag, a lipstick container, a hairpin and a notebook, all of which could be traced back to the victim. His most sensational find, however, and the clincher in the case, was a set of dentures which were categorically identified as having belonged to Mrs Durand-Deacon.

In Lewes Prison Haigh was well aware of the forensic evidence being amassed against him, but he remained optimistic. He was certain that he could escape the gallows by convincing a jury that he was in-

"Old Corpus Delicti"

Haigh chose his acid-bath method of disposing of his victims in the mistaken belief that it would protect him from prosecution. Even after his arrest, he boasted to fellow inmates at Dartmoor that he would never be convicted of the murder of Mrs Durand-Deacon because the police would never find her body. "Corpus delicti," he was fond of saying, "that's what'll save me. Get rid of the body and you've nothing to worry about." His persistence on this point earned him the prison nickname 'Old Corpus Delicti'.

Hard evidence

Haigh was wrong on two counts. Dr Keith Simpson did find several identification traces of Mrs Durand-Deacon's body, together with her false teeth; and Haigh totally misunderstood the expression corpus delicti. He assumed that corpus meant corpse, and indeed it is the Latin for body. But in legal parlance, it does not refer literally to the body of the deceased, but rather to the body of evidence. A body of fact, proof that the crime has been committed, must be sustantiated by the prosecution before a case can be established. It is not, however, essential for the victim's remains to be recovered.

Earlier case

If Haigh had done his research he would have known that in March 1948 James Camb, a ship's steward, had been convicted of murder without his victim's body ever being discovered. In October 1947, Camb had raped and strangled actress Gay Gibson aboard the SS Durban Castle. He had thrown his victim's body overboard and it was never recovered. Nevertheless, Camb was convicted on a mass of secondary forensic evidence. Bloody saliva on the victim's bed-linen, suggesting strangulation, urine staining on the mattress, consistent with the panic induced by an attack, and fingernail scratches on Camb's arms, all combined to convince a jury of his guilt.

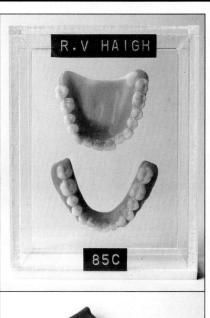

Haigh's acid bath left behind enough evidence to hang him. Mrs Durand-Deacon's dentures (top) were found in the still-acid soil of the yard. Made from acrylic resin, they were so well preserved that the dead woman's dentist was able to identify them immediately. Mrs Durand-Deacon's plastic handbag was also retrieved (above): inside was a notebook, metal pen, a lipstick holder and a compact.

Left: The search of the yard continues after Dr Simpson found three gallstones there, within minutes of his arrival.

sane, and on being told that Sir Maxwell Fyfe, the eminent barrister, was to represent him, Haigh was delighted. He wrote: "I'm very glad to see we have got old Maxy. He's no fool."

The trial of John Haigh for the murder of Mrs Durand-Deacon – that was the only charge ever brought against him – opened at Lewes Assizes on 18 July 1949, and lasted less than two days.

There was no real question as to whether Haigh had killed Mrs Durand-Deacon. The case rested on whether or not he was sane. The defence called Dr Henry Yellowlees, a consultant psychiatrist at St Thomas's Hospital, as an expert witness.

Doctor Yellowlees was no doubt an able man in his field, but he was a rotten witness. "In the case of pure paranoia," Yellowlees explained, "it really amounts, as it develops and gets a greater hold, to practically self-worship, and that is commonly expressed by the conviction in the mind of the patient that he is in some mystic way under the control of a guiding spirit which means infinitely more to him and is of infinitely greater authority than any human laws or rules of society."

Dr Yellowlees rambled on in this vein for some considerable time. He was frequently interrupted by both Sir Travers Humphreys, the judge, and Sir Hartley Shawcross, counsel for the prosecution, neither of whom had the faintest idea what he was talking about. As for the jury, he had lost them after the first few sentences and it took them only 13 minutes to return a verdict of 'guilty' on John George Haigh. Sir Travers Humphreys was equally speedy as he summoned the Black Cap and condemned him to death.

Haigh was taken to Wandsworth to await execution.

Chambers of Horrors

As the day of his execution approached, Haigh's apparently limitless poise began to crumble. He started to suffer from depression and complained of recurrent nightmares about blood. But despite this he maintained his sense of theatre. He bequeathed his favourite suit and tie to Madame Tussauds, ensuring himself his rightful place in the Chamber of Horrors, and he requested that the model of himself should show at least one inch of shirt cuff.

Then Haigh became concerned about the hanging itself. He contacted the prison governor, Major A.C.N. Benke, and re-

quested to rehearse his own execution. "My weight is deceptive," Haigh insisted, "I have a light springy step and I would not like there to be a hitch."

The governor turned down his request, assuring him that the executioner was highly experienced and that there would be no problems.

At 9 a.m. on the morning of 10 August, John Haigh was executed. His depression had left him and he was his old self, all swank and swagger, as he faced the gallows. That same day he was buried, as is the custom in cases of execution, inside the prison walls.

Victims murdered for their home

After his release from a jail sentence for fraud in 1943 Haigh returned to London. He got in contact with old friends, including William McSwan, who had once hired him to run an amusement arcade. Haigh arranged to meet McSwan in a Kensington pub and took him back to a basement flat in Gloucester Road. There he coshed him to death and dissolved his body in a tank of acid. Later that year he lured William McSwan's parents to the same flat and murdered them in the same cold-blooded fashion.

Left: Mrs Amy McSwan and her husband Donald were killed by Haigh in 1945. A year earlier he had killed their son William (below left). All three bodies were dissolved in acid.

Haigh forged papers so that he could sell William McSwan's house in Raynes Park, London.

Victim:

Dr Henderson and his wife Rosalie were the first of Haigh's victims to be killed in the Crawley workshop.

Police estimated that Haigh made about £4,000 by killing the McSwan family. He faked papers giving him power of attorney and sold off their property. This kept him going until February 1948, when he killed again.

The victims this time were Dr Archibald Henderson and his wife Rosalie, whom he met when looking around the house they were selling in Ladbroke Square. Haigh lured them to the workshop in Crawley and killed them both on the spot. By forging various documents he sold off property worth £8,000 during that year. He even took their red setter dog, which lived with him at Onslow Court.

The dishonourable schoolboy

There was no expression of pity for Haigh from the press, but there was a great deal of editorial speculation. How was it, they wondered, that an intelligent boy from a good home – his parents were members of the Plymouth Brethren – could grow into a monster like Haigh?

Religious bigots

Haigh himself went some way to answering them. He wrote from prison: "Although my parents were kind and loving, I had none of the joys, or the companionship, which small children usually have. From my earliest years, my recollection is of my father saying 'Do not' or 'Thou shalt not'. Any form of sport or light entertainment was frowned upon and regarded as not edifying. There was only condemnation and prohibition . . .

"It is true to say that I was nurtured on Bible stories but those mostly concerned with sacrifice. If by some mischance I did, or said, anything which my father regarded as improper, he would say: 'Do not grieve the Lord by behaving so.'"

On 24 July, five days after his trial ended, Haigh's mother sent him a 40th birthday card, but he rejected any suggestion that she visit him in Wandsworth Prison.

Eve of execution

On 9 August, the eve of his execution, Haigh wrote a letter to his parents. It began:

"My dearest Mum and Dad, Thank you for your very touching letter which I received this morning and which will, I suppose, be your last . . ." He went on to say that he had found parts of his upbringing very restrictive. "There was much that was lovely. . . . We cannot change the inscrutable predictions of the eternal . . . I, that is my spirit, shall remain earthbound for some time: my mission is not yet fulfilled . . ."

Haigh did not go on to explain what he thought his mission was, nor did he express any remorse for his terrible crimes. In the end, whatever was going on inside his mind went to the grave with him.

Some years later, it was Mrs Emily Haigh's turn to face death. A broken woman, she handed her son's letter to a friend, saying bitterly: "We used to despise the people in the village because we thought we were God's elect. "But we were not.""

Below: Haigh was sentenced to death on 18 July 1949 and hanged by executioner Albert Pierrepoint on 10 August. He secured Haigh's wrists with the 'special strap' he reserved for murderers of particular interest.

At the age of eight Haigh won a choral scholarship to Wakefield Grammar School. By 30 he was a convicted con-man and at the age of 40 he was hanged for murder.

lled for their money

Below: The basement of 38 Gloucester Road was where the McSwan family were killed one by one and their bodies dissolved.

Below: Police remove items from the basement after Haigh's startling confession to killing the McSwans and the Hendersons.

THE STAR

HE SMILED ON THE WAY TO COURT

HAIGH TO DIE
Jury Reach Their Verdict After Thirteen Minutes
Anything To Say? Nothing At All, He Replies

"*Star*" Reporter

JOHN GEORGE HAIGH WAS FOUND GUILTY AT THE SUSSEX ASSIZES AT LEWES THIS EVENING OF THE MURDER OF MRS OLIVIA DURAND-DEACON. HE WAS SENTENCED TO DEATH.

The jury took only 13 minutes to arrive at their verdict.

Asked whether he had anything to say before being sentenced to death, he said quietly, "Nothing at all."

The Poisonous Major

Herbert Armstrong was a small, dapper ex-soldier who had risen to the rank of Major during the First World War. Unhappily married, he planned to gain his freedom with the aid of arsenic. It was a plan which was to make him the only solicitor ever to be hanged in England.

Major Herbert Armstrong was a solicitor and a pillar of local society. But beneath his slight exterior, hidden passions raged. Passions which could only be satisfied by murder.

These days the Powys-Herefordshire border town of Hay-on-Wye is famed for its secondhand bookshops and annual literary festival. Seventy years ago, however, it was notorious as 'the home town of Major Armstrong, the wife poisoner' – the only solicitor in Britain to be hanged for murder.

Herbert Rowse Armstrong was the epitome of middle-class respectability. He was a solicitor with his own practice; Clerk to the Justices of Hay; a churchwarden; the Worshipful Master of the Masonic Lodge; commandant of the Territorial Army and, during Army service in the First World War, had risen to the rank of Major.

An MA graduate from Cambridge University, Armstrong was born in 1870 in Newton Abbot, Devon, and had moved to Hay a few years before the outbreak of the First World War. By 1920, two years after the Armistice, he appeared to have everything he wanted in life: his law practice was flourishing, and he owned a three-storey detached house with a large garden. His wife, Katherine, had nearly £2,500 capital of her own, which provided a useful income for luxuries such as her grand piano, on which she entertained the town's social elite at musical evenings.

But beneath the surface resentment simmered. Katherine Armstrong was a stickler for social etiquette, and ceaselessly nagged her husband. She would inform him loudly in company that it was his bath night, or that he had had "quite enough to drink" if he wanted another glass of wine. Their marriage had become passionless, and Armstrong tried to sublimate his sexual frustration into his one hobby – gardening. Indeed it may well have been his obsession for keeping his lawn free from dandelions – with an arsenic-based weedkiller – that sowed the seeds of his wife's early demise and, ultimately, his own.

Illicit affairs

The Major struck up liaisons with married women, yet he hardly had film-star looks. The thriller writer Edgar Wallace, who covered Armstrong's trial for a London news agency, described the Major as having "a small, round head with close-cropped, mouse-coloured hair; eyes set deeply in his head and rather close together; overhanging eyebrows were shaggy, and his projecting jaw was hidden by a heavy moustache."

These illicit affairs made Armstrong long to be free of the shackles of marriage. He began to formulate what he thought was a foolproof murder plot.

The large lawn provided the perfect cover. For some months he had been buy-

ing arsenic, both in compound and white powder form, as a weedkiller. He kept a reserve supply in the house and often amused himself by mixing his own compounds. The white powder, he noted, had no taste or odour and was colourless when dissolved in liquids.

He had the means and he had unlimited opportunity. All that remained was to await the right set of circumstances, and those came about rather unexpectedly.

In September 1920 Mrs Armstrong began to exhibit marked changes of mood. One day she would be melancholic, the next argumentative over household trivialities. The mood swings became more pronounced until the Major began to fear for her sanity. He called in the family doctor, Tom Hincks.

The doctor admitted her to nearby Barnwood Asylum "for observation". The asylum's medical superintendent diagnosed "peripheral neuritus"; and there she was to remain for the next four months. The Major engaged a housekeeper-governess to look after their three children, earning the town's sympathy for his stoicism.

When Mrs Armstrong was finally allowed home she made a new will, leaving all her private assets to her husband (this revoked an earlier will in which he would have benefited only slightly). Mrs Armstrong's decision to change her will couldn't have suited the Major's plan better! The ideal circumstances had arrived.

Armstrong wasted no time. A week later Mrs Armstrong was taken violently and painfully ill after a meal. Armstrong called in Dr Hincks, who treated Mrs Armstrong for gastritis aggravated by what he thought was a return to her neuritis.

Another attack

But no sooner had Mrs Armstrong recovered than she suffered a second attack. Again Hincks treated her for gastritis. That evening the Major gave his wife a glass (spiked?) of champagne to cheer her up. Indeed, Mrs Armstrong did rally briefly. But during the night her condition deterior-

A dose of arsenic

Until the middle of the 20th century arsenic was the classic poisoner's weapon. Its most common use was as a powder. Arsenic compounds are almost tasteless, and what little metallic sweetness there is can easily be masked by food.

Poisoning by arsenic, whether accidental or homicidal, became particularly prevalent during the 19th century. Arsenic compounds had many uses. White arsenic was used in sheep-dips and fly powders; sodium and potassium arsenite in sheep-dips, weedkillers and hide preservatives. Lead, calcium, manganese, magnesium and zinc arsenates were widely used as horticultural sprays and powders.

Acute arsenic poisoning requires the ingestion of a single large dose of more than 200 mg. The symptoms are those of severe gastroenteritis: pain and vomiting, then diarrhoea, followed by intense thirst, cramps and collapse. If the dose is large enough, death can occur within an hour.

Chronic poisoning – favoured by the domestic poisoner – results in loss of appetite, some vomiting, loss of weight and anaemia. Other symptoms include a pale speckling of the skin ('like raindrops'), loss of hair, brittle nails and itching of the hands and feet.

▶ ated and the Major summoned Dr Hincks.

The doctor did what he could to save her, but the 'gastritis' had done its deadly work. She died at 9.10 on the morning of 22 February 1921. Hincks wrote 'gastritis' on the death certificate.

Major Armstrong was in the clear, and very probably would have remained so had he not decided – either from recklessness or conceit over his success in disposing of his wife – to kill again.

At the funeral, attended by all the local dignitaries, the Major's sorrow as he stood at the graveside (he'd had a large ornate tombstone erected to his wife's memory) won the sympathy of the whole town. He told a friend: "The best and truest wife has gone to the Great Beyond and I am left without a partner and without a friend."

Every week during the spring and summer he placed flowers on the grave. Then he took a holiday – he deserved a break, everyone said – to France and Italy, returning with a new zest for life.

The grieving Major became the dashing Major. He took dancing lessons, entertained lavishly, smoked and drank freely. But he had brought back something more tangible than memories from his European jaunt – syphilis, a fact known only to Dr Tom Hincks.

Rival solicitor

Once back into his daily routine in Hay he began to be irked by a rival solicitor, Oswald Martin, who was not only taking away some of Armstrong's law business but was in dispute with him over some land he wanted to buy. Armstrong decided to solve the problem of Martin in the same way he'd solved the problem of his wife. He invited Martin to tea to "talk the matter over".

The Major laid on an inviting spread of cakes, sandwiches and buttered scones (one of which he'd spiked with white arsenic powder). Armstrong poured the tea and then, as they chatted amicably, handed Oswald Martin the poisoned scone with the apology: "Excuse fingers."

Oswald Martin ate every crumb and took his leave. Later that day he was taken ill with violent stomach pains; it so alarmed his wife that she immediately sent for Dr Hincks. Hincks might well have thought he was dealing with another case of severe gastritis but for the presence of Martin's father-in-law, John Davies, the local chemist. To his expert eye Martin's symptoms had all the hallmarks of arsenic poisoning. The only thing Martin had eaten that day that his wife hadn't was Major Armstrong's buttered scone.

And earlier that week a mysterious box of chocolates, addressed to Oswald Martin, had been delivered to the Martins' home by Royal Mail. The Martins had been entertaining friends at the time and Martin,

74

Above: Oswald Norman Martin was an up-and-coming young solicitor who was taking clients from Herbert Armstrong. Soon after taking tea with his rival, Martin fell seriously ill.

thinking the chocolates were from a grateful client who wished to remain anonymous, had handed them round. Mrs Martin's sister had eaten two – and had been violently ill a few hours later.

Dr Hincks and John Davies sent a specimen of Oswald Martin's urine and what was left of the chocolates to London for analysis. When Martin, still shaky from the attack, met Armstrong in the street a few days later, Armstrong coolly told him: "You must have eaten something which disagreed with you," adding, perhaps from boastful over-confidence, "and I have a feeling you will have another illness very similar."

Martin may have been reluctant at that stage to believe the worst of the town's respected Clerk to the Justices, but he nevertheless declined the Major's next invitation to have tea in the latter's new office. He also refused to meet Armstrong professionally.

Invitations to tea

In a less-conceited man, such rebuffs would have alerted caution. But no such warning bell rang in Armstrong's mind. On the contrary, he made no attempts to cover his tracks and continued to ply Martin with invitations to tea. For in the eyes of the townspeople the Major had done nothing more than "carry on" with certain married women.

Meanwhile, the results of the Home Office pathologist's tests had come through.

"1. Bottle. I have found arsenic in this bottle . . . in the amount of 1/33rd of a grain in the 17½ ounces of urine.

"2. Box. Two of the chocolates in this box had the appearance of having been tampered with. A cylindrical hole nearly ½

Above: Tests showed that Martin had been poisoned. His father-in-law, Mr Davies, was the town chemist, and he knew that Major Armstrong regularly bought arsenic-based weedkiller. Knowing of the ill-feeling between the two solicitors, he suspected that Armstrong might have poisoned Martin.

The torment of Mrs Armstrong

inch long has apparently been bored and filled with a white powder. This powder was found on analysis to be white arsenic to the extent of 2.12 grains. Two grains of white arsenic has been known to cause death in an adult."

Now Hincks and Davies knew the kind of diabolical mind of the would-be killer they were dealing with. Davies checked his chemist's poison register. Only one person in Hay had regularly signed for arsenic in fairly sizeable amounts – affable, mild-mannered Major Herbert Armstrong.

Suspicion alone, of course, was not enough to convict Armstrong. For though Scotland Yard regarded him as their prime suspect, they had no proof that he had sent the chocolates or poisoned the scone Martin had eaten; they were also wary of Armstrong's knowledge of criminal law and his friends in high places.

Identical symptoms

By then Dr Hincks recalled that Mrs Armstrong's death-bed symptoms were identical to Martin's. Had Mrs Armstrong died of arsenic poisoning? To find the answer, an exhumation application was sent to the Home Office. In the meantime Scotland Yard were confident they could make a charge of the attempted murder of Oswald Martin stick even though they had no direct evidence that Armstrong had administered the poison.

Two police officers went to Armstrong's office and made the arrest. The Major showed no signs of guilt or fear. "But you cannot do that," he said. "The charge is preposterous. Where is your warrant?" Armstrong knew that the officers would first have to apply to the Hay Justices

Below: Armstrong's wife had recently died, apparently of gastritis, but the symptoms could have been caused by arsenic. An exhumation was overseen by Sir Bernard Spilsbury (labelled No. 2) and the remains were found to contain arsenic.

In 1920 Katherine Armstrong was committed to a mental asylum for four months, during which time her husband sampled the pleasures of smoking, drinking and loose women. When his wife was released, the Major could not face returning to his old life, so he decided to get rid of Katherine for good.

13 February
Five days after her 48th birthday Mrs Armstrong suffered what appeared to be a severe gastric attack. Her symptoms included vomiting, severe stomach pain and muscular spasms.

16 February
She seemed to recover from the illness, but three days later, after eating a full dinner, she was stricken again. Doctor Tom Hincks noted that her normally sallow skin had turned a coppery colour and there were sores around her mouth.

22 January
At the insistence of her husband, Katherine Armstrong returned home from the asylum in January 1921. She was still weak and ill, which was an essential part of Major Armstrong's plan. He could poison her and any doctor would believe that she had died of the after-effects of her long illness.

18 February
Mrs Armstrong continued to suffer, alternately vomiting and having attacks of diarrhoea. Her pulse raced to 120 beats per minute, and by 18 February her arms and legs had become paralysed.

22 February
With the doctor's permission, the Major had been dosing his wife with some of her favourite homeopathic remedies. What the doctor did not know was that one of the ingredients was arsenic. Katherine Armstrong's lapse into unconsciousness and death was inevitable.

for a warrant to arrest him, and that he would have known if they had. And the delay while they did so would, he reasoned, give him time to safely dispose of the small packet he'd had in his jacket's inside pocket for days.

Armstrong was stunned when the officers immediately produced their warrant, signed by a higher authority than the Hay Justices, and escorted him to the local police cells. A search soon uncovered the packet. Asked what it was Armstrong said confidently: "Arsenic. I use it to kill the dandelions on my lawn."

The Major knew that would be hard for them to disprove; all the same the packet with its three grains (a lethal dose) of white powdered arsenic was a powerful indicator of his guilt – a point not overlooked by Mr Justice Darling at Armstrong's subsequent trial.

Meanwhile the Home Office's top pathologist, Sir Bernard Spilsbury, had been

sent to Hay to carry out the post-mortem on Mrs Armstrong's exhumed body. If no arsenic was found, the charge against Armstrong – the attempted murder of Martin – would, by implication, be weakened. It was a risk that had to be taken.

However, Spilsbury's painstaking examination of the partly decomposed corpse revealed three grains of arsenic. When Major Armstrong next appeared in court, he found himself facing the additional charge of murdering his wife.

Murder charge

The trial opened on 3 April 1922, at Hereford Assizes. Armstrong, who pleaded not guilty, was defended by Sir Edward Curtis-Bennett, a top advocate who had prosecuted all spies caught in Britain during the First World War. And the case against the Major was conducted by the Attorney-General, Sir Ernest Pollock (later to become Master of the Rolls). Armstrong, neatly dressed in highly polished brown shoes, fawn-coloured spats, brown tweed suit and brown tie, sat bolt upright with arms folded. He followed the evidence of every witness, his blue eyes rarely leaving their faces, apparently satisfying himself that the prosecution was not proving its case.

Only two days into the trial he told his warders at Gloucester Prison, where he was taken every night: "If this case were tried in Scotland, there could be no question that 'Not proven' would be the verdict."

But any lingering doubt that the 12 members of the jury might have had over his guilt vanished when Major Armstrong

went in the dock. Under the relentless questioning by Mr Justice Darling, Armstrong could offer no convincing explanation for the packet of arsenic in his pocket, nor for his efforts to conceal it during the police search.

And at that time, when moral attitudes were far less liberal than today's, the evidence by his doctor that he was being treated for syphilis badly damaged his character. Nor could Curtis-Bennett, for all his expertise, minimise the damning fact that Armstrong alone had possessed the means, the opportunity and the motive for murdering Katherine Armstrong. The jury returned a 'guilty' verdict after 48 minutes. Asked if he had anything to say, the Major replied: "Nothing."

On the morning of 31 May 1922 – the day of his execution at Gloucester Prison – he was given his tweed suit.

"Where's the collar?" he asked, adding quickly, "Oh! I quite understand."

Major Armstrong, who never confessed his guilt, refused an offer of £5,000 from a newspaper syndicate to tell the full story of his crimes. ☐

The final nail in Armstrong's coffin came when it was revealed that he had a venereal disease. To straight-laced jurors of the 1920s this was evidence of moral turpitude. They took less than an hour to find him guilty of the murder of his wife and he died on the gallows at Gloucester Prison.

Above and right: Major Armstrong arrives at Hereford Assizes for his trial for murder. It hardly seemed possible that this dapper, little man could have been a murderer. He spoke self-confidently in court, but he could not get around the fact that when arrested he was carrying a lethal dose of arsenic in his pocket, and there were 20 similar individually-wrapped doses at his home.

CARL COPPOLINO

Carl Coppolino, his wife Carmela and their two young children seemed like a classic all-American couple. Carl was a poor boy from New York who had made it out of the slums; Carmela was the daughter of a wealthy Italian-American family. Both were doctors, and they lived the good life on Florida's Gulf coast.

The Deadly
Anaesthetist

He was a smooth-looking, smooth-talking doctor, with a wealthy wife and two beautiful children. But Carl Coppolino was far from being the family man he appeared.

It was 6.20 a.m. on 28 August 1965 when Dr Juliette Karow arrived at the house of Carl and Carmela Coppolino in Longboat Key, a resort community on Florida's Gulf of Mexico coast. The Coppolinos were both qualified doctors who had moved from New Jersey a year earlier. Dr Karow had discussed the possibility of setting up in practice with Carmela when the newcomer had passed her Florida medical exams. But it was Carl who had called her out so early that August day.

Coppolino, an experienced anaesthetist who had been forced to give up work at the age of 31 due to heart trouble, greeted Dr Karow at the door. His words were simple: "She's dead."

Coppolino told Dr Karow that 32-year-old Carmela had complained of nausea and chest pains the evening before. During the night he had looked into her bedroom (the couple rarely shared a room). "I knew at once something was wrong," he said. "She didn't look natural." The concerned hus-

band felt for a pulse and found none. That was when he had called the doctor.

Dr Karow put the cause of death as coronary occlusion on the death certificate, and a couple of days later Carmela's body was flown north at her father's request to be buried in the family plot in Boonton, New Jersey. Carl was not at the funeral. He told the family his doctor had advised him that with his weak heart it might kill him.

Ex-lover makes trouble

And that was where the matter rested until Marjorie Farber began to make trouble. She'd had an affair with Coppolino in New Jersey, both before and after her husband died of a heart attack in 1963. The affair ended, but in August 1965 Marge, who was 14 years older than her ex-lover, decided to follow the Coppolinos south to Florida. She had even begun building a house on the plot next to theirs when she found that Carl had made a new friend.

A new wife

He was spending more and more time at the Maxwell Bridge Studio, where his regular partner was 38-year-old divorcée Mary Gibson. Many people at the studio believed the bridge partners were already lovers before Carmela died. But when Carl and Mary suddenly married just 40 days after Carmela's death, it was too much for Marge. She went to the Sarasota County police and told Sheriff Ross Boyer that not only had Carl murdered his wife, using an injection of the powerful anaesthetic succinylcholine chloride, which paralyses the muscles, but that he had also murdered her husband, Colonel William E. Farber, a retired army officer. The police were more inclined to believe her story because she was also implicating herself in her husband's killing.

A smiling **Carl Coppolino** is escorted from his **New Jersey** prison cell to court. The anaesthetist thought that he could easily evade the charge of murdering Colonel Farber.

The Coppolinos and Farbers had been neighbours in Middletown, New Jersey, from late 1962. In February 1963, shortly after he had had to give up his job at the Riverview Hospital, Carl, who had written a book on the use of hypnosis in anaesthesia, had hypnotised Marge to help her to stop smoking. Shortly afterwards they had started an affair.

Marge alleged that on the night of 29 July 1963 under post-hypnotic suggestion, she had taken a hypodermic that Carl had given her, and had started to inject her husband. "I couldn't stop myself," Marge claimed.

Neighbours and lovers

Carl and Carmela Coppolino were both Italian Americans. But Carl came from the slums of Brooklyn, while Carmela was the daughter of Carmelo Musetto, a wealthy doctor in Boonton, New Jersey. It was Carmela who persuaded Carl, then working his way through college, to drop his plan to become a scientist, and join her in studying medicine. They married in August 1956.

Threatening letters

Carl's promising career as an anaesthetist was cut short when he resigned from Riverview Hospital in January 1963. The reason given was heart trouble, but it seems that Carl was in fact asked to resign. A nurse at the hospital had been receiving threatening letters, and these were eventually traced to Carl. He claimed the woman had been cutting into his earnings, though he couldn't explain just how. It was the first sign that the handsome slum-boy-made-good wasn't all he seemed to be.

Affair with neighbour

A month after his enforced retirement and only weeks after the birth of his second child, Carl started an affair with Marjorie Farber. He would later be accused of using his skills as an anaesthetist to murder Marge's husband and his own wife.

Colonel William E. Farber had been a neighbour of the Coppolinos in New Jersey. He had ostensibly died of a heart attack.

Although their affair was long over, Marge Farber was so jealous of Carl's marriage to his second wife Mary that she was prepared to incriminate herself to get her revenge on him.

"It was absolutely over and beyond my own free will." Then, unable to go through with it, Marge had phoned Carl. The doctor allegedly left his wife in bed, came over to the Farbers' house, and finished the job himself, first drugging his victim, and then using a pillow to smother the unfortunate Colonel.

Police investigations proved that Coppolino had indeed obtained a supply of succinylcholine chloride shortly before Colonel Farber's death, and again just five weeks before Carmela died. Carl claimed that in the first case it had been to dispose of a troublesome dog, and that in the second he was planning some research into a way of measuring the concentration of the drug in the blood during surgery. But to the police it looked highly suspicious.

Wife's body exhumed

Carmela Coppolino's body was exhumed on 16 December 1965 and was given to Dr Milton Helpern, New York City's distinguished chief medical examiner, for post-mortem. There was no obvious cause of death. Helpern found the young woman's heart to be completely normal. Then he discovered a tiny puncture mark in her left buttock, consistent with the use of a hypodermic needle. Immediately tissue samples were sent to toxicologist Dr Joseph Umberger for analysis.

The obvious thing to do was to test for the presence of succinylcholine chloride but there was no such test. There was no difficulty in detecting succinic acid and choline, the metabolites of succinylcholine chloride, but both substances are present

naturally in the human body; it was also impossible to determine whether there was an excess, as there were no clear guidelines on how much was normal. In fact the anaesthetic drug, based on the South American Indian poison curare, appeared to be the perfect murder weapon.

Undaunted, Dr Umberger set about attempting to devise a test. For six months he processed samples from Carmela's brain and other organs and from the injection site in her buttock. Finally in June 1966 he was able to make an initial report stating that he had succeeded in isolating both succinic acid and choline. Marge Farber was looking increasingly credible.

Consequently on 14 July her husband's body was exhumed from Arlington Cemetery, and also handed over to Milton Helpern for post-mortem. Colonel Farber's body had been in the ground too long to be tested for succinylcholine chloride, but the medical examiner found what he thought was more direct evidence of foul play. The cricoid cartilage in the larynx was fractured in two places. Helpern reported that Colonel Farber had been strangled.

Carl Coppolino was arrested for the murder of William E. Farber on 23 July 1966. Four days later he was in hospital under guard having suffered a heart seizure, when the police informed him he had also been indicted for the murder of his wife.

There would be two trials – one in Freehold, New Jersey, for the murder of William Farber, the other in Naples, Florida, for the killing of Carmela Coppolino. Both juries would hear testimony from Marge Farber and a range of expert witnesses, especially Milton Helpern. At both trials Carl Coppolino would have the services of star lawyer F. Lee Bailey, already a nationally known figure just six years after leaving law school. But the two juries would reach totally different conclusions.

At Freehold Court Coppolino convinced the jury that his treatment of Colonel Farber on the night of 29/30 July 1963 had been of the highest medical standard. He had given a tranquilliser to the patient and then Pronestol to improve his uneven heartbeat. But he had withdrawn from the case the next day, and demanded a written release from Marge, when she and her husband both rejected his advice that the Colonel should be taken to hospital. The neck damage noted by Dr Helpern could have occurred during the exhumation. Defence expert Dr Spelman supported Coppolino's version by saying: "There was sufficient arteriosclerosis in Colonel Farber's coronary arteries to account for his death." So perhaps he'd had a heart attack after all.

Acquitted of first murder

The jury in Freehold took just four-and-a-half hours to decide to acquit Carl Coppolino of the murder of Colonel Farber. Free on bail, he returned to Florida with Mary, and the couple went off for a holiday.

Both Bailey and Carl himself thought the Florida charge would be easier to beat. There was no alleged eye-witness and Marge's testimony would only amount to her suspicions and what she claimed was her concern for the new Mrs Coppolino. The prosecution's entire case rested on the testimony of the experts and particularly on Dr Joseph Umberger's newly devised tests for a substance many experts believed to be untraceable. But the jury in

Famous New York pathologist Milton Helpern was sure of Coppolino's guilt, but most unusually there were grave doubts about the quality of his evidence.

the small town of Naples, Florida, was ready to hand everyone a surprise.

Whether Carl Coppolino was guilty or not of murdering his wife, any review of the prosecution medical evidence must leave some doubt over just what it proved. Succinylcholine chloride breaks down extremely rapidly in the body. Hence the problems in detecting the substance. Dr Umberger had found succinic acid in samples taken from Carmela Coppolino's brain, but none at the injection site. Defence experts on the other hand declared that, if there had been an injection of the drug, the evidence would have been found at the injection site, and that the succinic acid in the brain was almost certainly naturally occurring.

Bailey put it to the toxicologist that the

MONMOUTH COUNTY JAIL

Mary Coppolino (right) stood by Carl through both trials and subsequent imprisonment. Coppolino himself was released in 1979 (below) after serving 12 years for second degree murder.

autopsy report had been altered by Dr Helpern to make it look worse for Coppolino. Umberger then admitted he had only ever said it was 'possible' that Carmela Coppolino had been injected with succinylcholine chloride. It was, he said, on Dr Helpern's insistence that the word 'possible' was deleted from the final report on the case. "Dr Helpern didn't like 'possible'," Umberger admitted.

Here, then, was medical evidence that had apparently been doctored by the prosecution's star witness to make it look more certain than it really was. Bailey believed he'd scored a knock-out blow on his opponent Dr Milton Helpern. In fact, so certain was the lawyer that he'd succeeded in making the prosecution's scientific case look like a put-up job, that he decided not to put Carl on the stand to deny the accusation himself. Perhaps this was what told against him, because at 9.30 a.m. on 28 April 1967 the jury brought a verdict of guilty.

Second degree murder

Even then it didn't seem a wholehearted decision. The all-male jury found Coppolino guilty not of premeditated murder, as charged, but of second degree murder, which meant he didn't face the death penalty. In a case of alleged poisoning a verdict of unpremeditated murder seems almost nonsensical.

Nevertheless, Coppolino was sentenced to life imprisonment, the maximum possible term for second degree murder, and ultimately served 12 years, before being paroled on 16 October 1979 in recognition of his good conduct in prison. Mary Coppolino, who never doubted his innocence, had campaigned long and hard for his freedom. She was there to greet him at the prison gates on his release.   □